UNDERSTANDING TOURISM

UNDERSTANDING TOURISM

B.S. Badan
Harish Bhatt

Commonwealth

[The responsibility for the facts stated, conclusions reached and plagiarism, if any, in this book is entirely that of the Author. And the Publisher bears no responsibility for them, whatsoever.]

Understanding Tourism

First Published : 2007

ISBN 81-311-0076-6

Published by :

Ajay Verma
For COMMONWEALTH PUBLISHERS
4831/24, Prahlad Street,
Ansari Road, Darya Ganj,
New Delhi - 110002
Ph. : 23272541, 23257835
Fax : 91- 011- 23257835
e-mail : campusbooks@hotmail.com

Printed at :
Roshan Offset Printers
Delhi

PREFACE

Tourism can be defined as the act of travel for the purpose of recreation, and the provision of services for this act. It is a service industry, comprising a number of tangible and intangible components. The tangible elements include transportation systems—air, rail, road, water and now, space; hospitality services, accommodation, foods and beverages, tours, souvenirs; and related services such as banking, insurance and safety and security. The intangible elements include: rest and relaxation, culture, escape, adventure, new and different experiences.

Travel and tourism is a major industry in the world and is at the top of the league of invisible earners of foreign currency. Many sovereignties, along with their respective countries and states, depend heavily upon travel expenditures by foreigners as a source of taxation and income for the enterprises that sell services to these travellers. Consequently the development of tourism is often a strategy employed either by a non-governmental organization or a governmental agency to promote a particular region for the purpose of increasing commerce through exporting goods and services to non-locals.

During recent years the tourism industry has witnessed unprecedented growth. Increasing consumer demand for educational and participatory travel experiences has resulted in a variety of specialty niche markets such as ecotourism, cultural-heritage tourism, and agritourism. New paradigms link strategic tourism planning with sustainable development.

The leisure and tourism industry is one of the leading global economic activities, a multi-billion-dollar industry with

700 million international travellers per year around the world. Tourism is a motor for employment and income creation and, especially in poor countries, a vehicle for development. But today it is not sufficient to simply create employment without regard for the quality of jobs and the social and environmental effects of tourism in vulnerable areas. A growing number of organizations, including the tourism industry leadership, are increasingly conscious of the risks and are adopting a more responsible attitude.

The present publication provides an authoritative look at how to manage travel and tourism industry in a better way. It introduces the complexities of the tourism system so that they will be better positioned to eventually assume the managerial challenges and responsibilities in a diverse and challenging industry. The latest advancements in tourism theory and thinking, retaining the thoroughness of content, diversity of applications, regional and international issues, economic significance, tourism operators and the role of technology in the tourism industry etc. are also described elaborately. Numerous regional and global case studies and examples are included to provide an appropriately broad geographic context. This work will be highly informative and useful to students, researchers, policy makers, managers and working groups of travel and tourism industry.

B.S. Badan
Harish Bhatt

CONTENTS

1 INTRODUCTION

Introduction

At first glance, the value of another text on destination marketing may seem limited. However, destination branding is not just another aspect of destination marketing and its study is no mere academic bandwagon. Rather it is a belated acknowledgement of a fundamental transformation in the marketing of destinations—and beyond this –in the marketing of places. Such has been the explosion of interest in destinational branding that a collection such as this, bringing together practitioners and academics, is long overdue—the practice of place branding has far outpaced the extent to which it has been written about in the public realm. Arguably, far from actively engaging with destination branding issues, many have shied away from the topic—arguing that places are too complex to include in branding discussions since they have too many stakeholders and too little management control, have underdeveloped identities and are not perceived as brands by the general public. And yet, destination branding is one of today's 'hottest' topics among place marketers—from Switzerland and New Zealand to Hawaii and Costa Rica (Piggott, 2001).

Indeed, place are potentially the world's biggest tourism brands. Choice of holiday destination is a significant lifestyle indicator for today's aspirational consumers and the places where they choose to spend their increasingly squeezed vacation time and hard earned income have to be emotionally appealing with high conversational and celebrity value. The World Tourism Organization talks about this in terms of seeing destinations as tomorrow's fashion items, suggesting that : 'The next century will mark the emergence of tourism destinations as a fashion accessory. The choice of holiday destination will help define the identity of the traveller and, in an increasingly homogeneous world, set him [sic] apart from the hordes of other tourists' (Lurham, 1998 : 13).

As style and status indicators, destinations can offer the same consumer benefits as other more highly branded lifestyle accouterments such as cars, perfumes, watches and clothes. All are used to communicate, reflect and reinforce associations, statements and group memberships and, in the same way, tourists use 'their trips as expressive devices to communicate messages about themselves to peers and observers' (Clarke, 2000 : 330). Travel for leisure is often a highly involving experience, extensively planned, excitedly anticipated and fondly remembered. Souvenirs and 'props' trigger and display those experiences—photographs, videos and 'wish you were here' postcards are shared with friends and relatives, and logo-emblazoned merchandise and luggage labels, proclaim 'been there, done that' to any observers who care to notice (Clarke, 2000; Westwood, 2000).

Tapping into the power of such emotional appeal, tourism destinaton brands are also beginning to reach beyond the tourism industry. Many of those brands at the leading edge of destination marketing are seeking to position themselves as place brands, whereby whole countries, states and regions are embarking on brand-building initiatives that are inclusive of tourism and economic development. While the task is by no means easy, the rewards are enormous and, drawing on many case studies from the leading edge of destination marketing practice, the chapters in this collection evidence this view. Written by an international mixture of practitioners and academics, the subsequent chapters address a varied range of destinations, each at a different stage of development and each grappling with the challenges presented by destination branding. What is striking, however, is the commonality of their approaches to the process and the recurring themes that emerge as key to destination brand building.

The reader should not, therefore, be surprised that several of the chapters reiterate these themes. Instead, the collection reflects the fact that these are the crucial issues facing contemporary destination marketers—whether their activities are at national, regional, state or city level. The ways in which each destination seeks to tackle such issue will, of course, depend on local circumstances, finances and resources—there will always be local solutions to global challenges. However, the contributions included here suggest that there are common elements to these solutions—key issues and activities which every marketer seeking to achieve successful destination branding must address. These include : the often destructive role of politics in crafting brands; the essential role of inclusive, comprehensive and ongoing market research in identifying and creating the brand values; the need to build alliances and partnerships across all the stakeholder groups; and the value of 'band champions' who have the vision, commitment and 'staying' power to drive the brand development. Finally, the reader is left with the clear message that the success of any destination brand depend on the extent to which it truly 'lives' for tourists. To really achieve destination branding, marketers must be in the business of delivering impactful experiences, not merely constructing a clever brand identity on paper with slick slogans and brand logos. The world's most successful destination brands have achieved this and those who seek to emulate them must follow the same principles, many of which are articulated and evidenced in the following chapters.

Destination Branding in Perspective

The book is divided into two parts—the first focuses on destination branding perspectives while the second presents four detailed explorations of successful destination branding initiatives, together with a discussion of on-line branding opportunities. Following this introduction, Migel Morgan and Annette Pritchard contextualize destination branding, suggesting that it offers marketers the opportunity to counter one of the greatest dilemmas facing destinations—the sheer substitutability of their offerings. As Morgan and Pritchard discuss, however, putting destination branding into practice is no easy talks and destinations face a number of challenges which each have the potential to derail the best branding initiatives. As their examples of Morocco and Israel suggest, political pressures. External environmental changes and product issues all have to be successfully combated if a destination brands is to prosper and grow. That said, successful branding brings significant rewards and the remainder of their chapter discusses how strong destination brands can be built around the concepts of 'wish you were here' appeal and celebrity value, focusing on a range of examples including Spain, New Zealand, Australia and Oregon, USA. They argue that brand winners are those places rich in emotional meaning, which have great conversational value and high anticipation for tourists, while band losers have little meaning, status or emotional pull.

Simon Anholt, in his wide-ranging and thought-provoking, exploration of 'provenance' in branding, then illustrates how successful 'nation' brands provide trust, quality and lifestyle connotations that consumers can readily purchase, explore and associate with themselves. In an eclectic discussion, Anholt demonstrates how demonstrates how strategy which highlighted Wales' natural environment its potential as an off season, short-break destination.

Shane Crockett and Leiza Wood shift the focus from nation to state branding in their detailed analysis of the Western Australian Tourism Commission's (WATC) approach. This strategy, based on intensive consumer research, government-industry partnerships and infrastructural developments, demonstrates the value not merely of developing a tourism but a state-wide brand. This chapter provides a rich source of good practice for state branders everywhere through its discussion of the challenges of the state's macroenvironment, its repositioning task, the development of Brand Western Australia (BWA) and the measures adopted to evaluate its marketing and partnership strategies. As Crockett and Wood demonstrate, successful destination branding must embrace a host of activities, including infrastructural development, product enhancement, protection against environmental degradation, changes in organizational culture, and promotional partnership—all based on intensive market research to identify consumer desires. This case study of BWA demonstrates that, when combined with the development of a distinctive, broad visual language and strong creative promotional executions, these activities can provide the platform for a successful destination brand.

Continuing the theme of state branding. Jan Slater examines the brand-building success story of Louisiana, a state that has managed to create a powerful travel destination brand in perhaps the most demanding consumer market in the world—the USA. Such success is no mean task in a country where annual state government tourism promotional spending exceeds half a billion dollars in an effort to attract a domestic audience accounting for over a billion tourism trips. As Slater explains, the travel industry, once known for its 'wallpaper' advertising is wholeheartedly embracing 'branding to order' to communicate and emphasize the 'feel' and 'personality' of a place. Destinations are thus seeking to become experiences as opposed to merely a place to spend time. Louisiana (like many other destinations), with its colourful multicultural history, has many attractions to recommend itself to the would-be visitor. It is its successful brand identity, however, which has positioned Louisiana as one of the fastest growing tourism destinations in the USA. Significantly, the process has been underpinned by the development of a strong advertising agency—government tourism office partnership. The former, through their insightful 'mining' of existing consumer research, were able to develop a strong, differentiating, brand proposition and identity for the state which has remained largely unchanged since its conception in 1993. As Slater highlights, however, brand proposition need to be matched by efficient and effective media exposure and strong budgets if they are to succeed.

This is a point made abundantly clear in the penultimate chapter, written by Graham Brown, Laurence Chalip, Leo Jago and Trevor Mules, which considers the relationship between events and destination branding from a number of perspectives. After discussing the growing importance of event tourism, the authors examine the nature of destination image in the context of conceptual and applied frameworks before evaluating the status of the relationship between event management and tourism by reporting recent insight gained in Australia. The chapter reports findings from a research project that is focusing exclusively on the role of events in destination branding before considering the implications of the Sydney Olympic Games on Brand Australia. Brown, Chalip, Jago and Mules provide a richly researched insight into how Australia's destination marketers shrewdly harnessed the global appeal of the Olympic Games to promote not only Sydney's but, the whole of Australia's tourism image to the world. The case study clearly demonstrates how the 'best ever games' was used to strategically advance Brand Australia and leaves the reader in no doubt as to the value of hosting the global event.

The collection concludes with an examination of the opportunities and challenges that the Internet offers destination branders. Such is the significance of the web in this area that most of the earlier contributions, discussed above, also draw attention to the role of the Internet and some of the featured destinations are building brands which heavily feature the internet. In Adrian Plamer thus focuses on the impacts emerging high-speed data transmission technologies such as the Web, e-commerce and m-commerce will have on destination branding. Significantly, he shows that the Internet facilitates both the creation of strong, highly branded sites and a much stronger presence for individual tourism suppliers. Such a synergy should go some way to bridging the gap between destination branding and an industry which sometimes fails to see the value and impact such umbrella activities have on their businesses. In fact internet proliferation, audience splintering and an increasingly techno-literate society are combining to make Web-based destination brading increasingly critical. While the Web creates challenges it also opens up opportunities—of interactive advertisements, smart web sites and e-consumers seeking engagement and engaging promotions (Morgan, Pritchard and Abbott, 2001).

Given that the Web offer each individual tourism supplier the opportunity to directly position themselves and communicate interactively with potential consumers, challenges to destination-branding initiatives (and to the role of the destination-marketing organizations themselves) will only increase without partnership, communication and co-operation. As we case our way into the twenty-first century, it cannot be denied that the role of destination branding is critical and will become ever more so. In a world dominated by change and celebrity, in which the virtual world will become the focus of much marketing activity, those destinations which can successfully 'brand' the gap between suppliers and consumers will be today's and particularly tomorrow's brand winners. One inescapable conclusion from this collection is that there must be much more detailed case-study based investigations into destination branding—especially those evaluating the long-term success of such activities. Indeed, this is also true of tourism and branding in general—we need much more detailed knowledge of just how consumers interact with brands in the world's fastest growing industry.

2 ANATOMY OF TOURISM

2.1 Defining Tourism

† **1** Which of the following authors is known for the earliest published attempt to define tourism?

A W. Hunziker and K.Krapf in *Allgemeine Fremdenverkehrslehre* □
B L.J. Lickorish and A.G. Kershaw in *The Travel Trade* □
C A.J. Norval in *The Tourist Industry* □
D F.W. Ogilvie in *The Tourist Movement* □

*† **2** Insert the missing words (*business, environment, not more, staying*) in the definition of tourism by the World Tourism Organization (1993) below:

Tourism comprises the activities of persons travelling to and

A......................in places outside their usual

B......................for C......................than one consecutive year for leisure, D......................and other purposes.

† **3** A distinction may be drawn between **conceptual** and **technical** definitions of tourism. Which are used in

A surveys? ....
B legislation? ....

† **4** Which of the following is an essential element of any **technical** definition of tourism?

A Expenditure ☐
B Mode of transport ☐
C Purpose of trip ☐
D Type of accommodation ☐

*† 5 Insert the missing words (*destination, regions, tourist, tourists*) in the description of tourism as a system by Australian author Neil Leiper (1979) below :

The elements of the system are
A......................generating
B......................transit routes,
C......................regions and a
D......................industry.

*† 6 Which of the following statements is **true**?
A Tourism is synonymous with travel. ☐
B All tourism is a leisure activity. ☐
C Tourism includes travel to work. ☐
D Much tourism involves discretionary use of time and money. ☐

*† 7 Which of the following statements is **false**?
In comparison with international tourism, in many countries domestic tourism is :
A much larger ☐
B growing faster ☐
C less regulated ☐
D better documented ☐

† 8 Which of the following are to be regarded as tourists according to the recommendations of the World Tourism Organization?
A Air crews staying overnight at the destination. ☐
B Consultants remunerated directly by clients at the destination. ☐
C Members of the armed forces travelling between their country of origin and duty station. ☐
D Students travelling between their home and institution at the beginning of each term. ☐

† **9** Which of the following are **not** to be regarded as tourists according to the recommendations of the World Tourism Organization?

A Diplomats travelling between their country of origin and duty station. ☐

B Guests attending weddings and funerals. ☐

C Pilgrims. ☐

D Those visiting friends and relatives. ☐

*† **10** Link each term in the first column with one term in the second to show the most meaningful relationships :

1 Balance of payments A Tourism industry

2 Resorts B Tourist destinations

3 Tourist facilities C International tourism

1st column	1	2	3
2nd column			

2.2 Studying Tourism

Which academic discipline contributes an understanding of the following?

*† **1** Supply and demand relationships in tourism

....

*† **2** Spatial dimensions and relationships in tourism

....

*† **3** Motivations in tourism

....

*† **4** Government roles and relationships in tourism

....

*† **5** Social impacts of visitors on communities

....

what are the following called?

† 6 Study of bathing and mineral waters and their healing effects

....

† 7 Study of the interrelationships between living organisms and the environment

....

† 8 Statistical study of populations

....

*† 9 Study of weather

....

*† 10 Representation of surface feature of an area on a map

....

2.3 Types and Forms of Tourism

*† 1 The term 'common interest tourism' describes
- A group travel by people with the same interests ☐
- B group visits between 'twinned' towns only ☐
- C a synonym for visits to friends and relatives ☐
- D visits with a purpose significantly shared by the visitor and the visited ☐

*† 2 The term 'cultural tourism' means trips and visits
- A concerned with soil utilization ☐
- B by the educated and discerning ☐
- C motivated by cultural interests ☐
- D in pursuit of learning and scholarship ☐

*† 3 The term 'domestic tourism' denotes
- A travel by indigenous population of a country ☐
- B journeys with stays in private households ☐
- C travel within one's own country ☐
- D coastal travel between ports of a country ☐

*† 4 The term 'ethnic tourism' refers to
- A travel by particular racial groups ☐
- B visiting particular racial groups ☐

C travel by indigenous people ☐
D visits for ethnic reunion ☐

*† 5 The term 'health tourism' is concerned with
A treatment of travel-related diseases ☐
B quarantines imposed by heath authorities ☐
C visits to health resorts and establishments ☐
D travel by medical and nursing personnel ☐

*† 6 The term 'incentive tourism' denotes
A travel rewarded by commissions ☐
B travel that has been paid for by a firm as a reward to employees ☐
C travel stimulated by inducements ☐
D travel using vouchers to cover spending *en route* ☐

*† 7 The term 'international tourism' applies to
A most travel between countries ☐
B all travel for which passports are required ☐
C travel between countries with different currencies ☐
D travel between countries with different languages ☐

*† 8 The term 'mass tourism' refers to tourism
A in which large numbers take part ☐
B which is promoted through mass media ☐
C exceeding carrying capacity of a destination ☐
D consisting of travel to mass meetings ☐

*† 9 The term 'rural tourism'
A is synonymous with agricultural tourism ☐
B describes travel by residents of rural areas ☐
C refers to travel to countryside destinations ☐
D means travel between rural destinations ☐

*† 10 The term 'urban tourism' describes
A business travel ☐
B travel by residents of urban areas ☐
C travel to town and city destinations ☐
D travel between towns and cities ☐

2.4 Propensities, Determinants, Motivations

† 1 In a country with a population of 55 million, 33 million people took 44 million holiday (vacation) trips in a year. What was

A the net holiday (vacation) propensity? ....
B the gross holiday (vacation) propensity? ....
C the holiday (vacation) frequency? ....

*† 2 What is single most important determinant of the holiday (vacation) propensity in a country?

A Car ownership ☐
B Second home ownership ☐
C Standard of living ☐
D Urbanization ☐

*† 3 Available evidence suggests that holiday (vacation) propensity generally increases with

A age ☐
B size of household ☐
C unemployment ☐
D level of education ☐

*† 4 Which of the following are demand determinants (D) and which are supply determinants (S) in tourism?

A Availability of tourism accommodation ....
B Degree of urbanization ....
C Level of air fares ....
D Occupational distribution of the population ....

*† 5 An increase in the value of a country's currency against all other currencies is generally likely to

A decrease the country's residents' travel abroad ☐
B have no effect on residents' travel abroad ☐
C decrease arrivals from other countries ☐
D have no effect on arrivals ☐

† 6 The push-pull theory was originally developed to explain

A migration ☐
B motivation to work ☐

C need for social interaction ☐
D why people travel ☐

† 7 Which of the following is true of Maslow's needs theory?

A It was developed to explain tourist behaviour. ☐
B It applies to leisure but not to work behaviour. ☐
C It states that human needs as motivators form a hierarchy. ☐
D It suggests that one has to satisfy fully the needs at one level before moving on to the next. ☐

† 8 In his personality theory of tourist behaviour, American researcher Stanley Plog distinguishes between types of traveller. What are the extremes called?

A One with a preference for exploration and inquisitiveness, exotic destinations and unstructured vacations is called

....

B One who is not adventurous and wants security, prefers familiar destinations, tourist areas and package tours is called

....

† 9 Which of the following show primarily sunlust motivations (S) and which show primarily wanderlust motivations (W), as defined by American author H. P. Gray (1970)?

A An African on a sightseeing tour of Europe ....
B An American on a safari in Africa ....
C A German on a beach holiday (vacation) on the Italian Riviera ....
D A Scotsman on a skiing holiday (vacation) in the French Alps ....

† **10** The term 'conspicuous consumption', as defined by American economist Thorstein Veblen (1899), refers to purchases

A of consumer good and services generally ☐

B of consumer durables ☐

C which satisfy a physical need ☐

D which satisfy a psychological need ☐

2.5 Describing People

Note : This test may be attempted with or without reference to the following list : alien, citizen, commuter, day visitor, emigrant, excursionist, exile, expatriate, guest worker, national, nomad, overnight visitor, (same) day visitor, stayover visitor, tourist.

What term describes a person who

*† **1** is a member of a state by birth or naturalization?

....

*† **2** moves voluntarily away from his/her native country to take up permanent residence in another country?

....

† **3** lives voluntarily away from his/her country of citizenship?

....

*† **4** is compelled by political or other circumstances to live away from his/her native country?

....

*† **5** is a visitor staying at least one night in the place visited?

....

*† **6** is a visitor not staying overnight in the place visited?

....

*† **7** is not a citizen of the country of his/her residence?

....

† **8** moves temporarily to another country for employment?

....

† **9** lives a wandering life?

....

*† **10** travels regularly between his/her place of residence and work?

....

2.6 Tourism Concepts

Underline which is the wider concept in each of the following pairs :

† 1	A common interest tourism	B visits to friends and relatives
*† 2	A destination	B resort
† 3	A discretionary income	B disposable income
*† 4	A domestic tourism	B internal tourism
*† 5	A domestic tourism	B national tourism
† 6	A farm tourism	B rural tourism
*† 7	A health tourism	B spa tourism
*† 8	A leisure	B recreation
*† 9	A tourist	B visitor
*† 10	A traveller	B visitor

2.7 Tourism Synonyms

Give a synonym for each of the following terms :

† **1** citizen

....

*† **2** excursionist

....

*† **3** industrialized countries

....

*† **4** package tour

....

† **5** permanent residence

....

† **6** responsible tourism

....

*† **7** service industries

....

*† **8** Third World countries

....

† **9** tour operator

....

† **10** tourism sector

....

2.8 Tourism Opposites

Give the opposite of each of the following terms :

*† **1** business travel

....

*† **2** domestic tourism

....

*† **3** emigrant

....

*† **4** group travel

....

*† 5 inbound tourism

....

*† 6 inclusive tour

....

*† 7 main holiday (vacation)

....

*† 8 overnight visit

....

*† 9 tourist generating area

....

*† 10 urban tourism

....

2.9 US versus UK Language **US/UK**

Give the UK equivalents of the following American terms :

1 auto rental

....

2 automobile

....

3 campground

....

4 lodging industry

....

5 motor home

....

6 price/rate hike

....

7 railroad

....

8 vacation

....

9 vacation home

....

10 vacation trip

....

2.10 The Language North of the Border **UK**

Give the Scottish term for :

1 a deep narrow valley, usually forming the course of a stream

....

2 a wide valley or low-lying flat land bounded by hills or high ground

....

3 a narrow channel between two islands or an island and the mainland

....

4 a lake or arm of the sea, especially if bounded by steep sides or partly landlocked

....

5 a mountain peak

....

6 a mountain over 3,000 ft. (914m) high

....

7 a promontory or headland in Scotland

....

8 an area of coastal water, *e.g.* arm of the sea, an estuary

....

9 a bridge

....

10 a one-room cottage or hut used as a frameworks' or shepherds' shelter, nowadays also for walkers

....

ANSWERS

2.1 Defining Tourism and Tourists

1 D F.W. Ogilvie (*in The Tourist Movement,* Staples Press, 1933; *The Tourist Industry* was published by Pitman in 1936, *Allgemeine Fremdenverkehrslehre* by Polygraphischer Verlag, Zurich in 1942, *The Travel Trade* by Practical Press in 1958)

2 A staying
B environment
C not more
D business
} See World Tourism Organization (1993), *Recommendations on Tourism Statistics*, Madrid : WTO

3AB Technical definitions are used in both.

4 C Purpose of trip (which distinguishes between tourism and other travel and between particular forms of tourism)

5 A tourists
B regions
C destination
D tourist
} Leiper, N. (1979) The Framework of Tourism: Towards a Definition of Tourism, Tourist, and the Tourist Industry, *Annals of Tourism Research*, 6 (4), 390-407

6 D Much tourism involves discretionary use of time and money. (See Question 2 above.)

7 D Domestic tourism is not better documented.

8 A Air crews staying overnight at the destination (See WTO, *Recommendations on Tourism Statistics*)

9 A Diplomats travelling between their country of origin and duty station (as above).

10

1st column	1	2	3
2nd column	C	B	A

2.2 Studying Tourism

1. Economics
2. Geography
3. Psychology
4. Politics
5. Sociology
6. Balneology
7. Ecology
8. Demography
9. Meteorology
10. Topography

2.3 Types and Forms of Tourism

1. D visits with a purpose significantly shared by the visitor and visited (including B and C but not confined to them)
2. C trips and visits motivated by cultural interests
3. C travel within one's own country
4. D visits for ethnic reunion (also visits to places inhabited by indigenous and other exotic people)
5. C visits to health resorts and establishments
6. B travel paid for by a firm as a reward to employees (also, *e.g.,* to dealers and agents and often including spouses)
7. A most travel between countries
8. A tourism in which large numbers take part
9. C travel to countryside destinations
10. C travel to town and city destinations

2.4 Propensities, Determinants, Motivations

1 A Net propensity = 60% $\left(\frac{33 \text{ million}}{55 \text{ million}}\right) \times 100$

B Gross propensity =80% $\left(\frac{44 \text{ million}}{55 \text{ million}}\right) \times 100$

C Frequency = 1.33 $\left(\frac{44 \text{ million}}{33 \text{ million}}\right)$

2 C Standard of living (commonly measured by GDP/GNP per capita)

3 D level of education

4 A Supply/determinant
B Demand determinant
C Supply determinant
D Demand determinant

5 C decrease arrivals from other countries

6 A migration

7 C Human needs as motivators form a hierarchy.

8 A allocentric
B psychocentric

9 A Wanderlust
B Wanderlust
C Sunlust
D Sunlust
} Gray, H.P. (1970) *International Travel-International Trade*, Lexington: Health Lexington Books

10 D It refers to purchases which satisfy a psychological need. (See Veblen, T. (1899) *The Theory of the Leisure Class*, New York :.Mentor, 1953)

2.5 Describing People

1 citizen/national
2 emigrant
3 expatriate
4 exile/refugee
5 tourist/overnight visitor/stayover visitor
6 (same) day visitor/excursionist
7 alien
8 guest worker
9 nomad
10 commuter

2.6 Tourism Concepts

1 A common interest tourism
2 A destination
3 B disposable income
4 B internal tourism
5 B national tourism
6 B rural tourism
7 A health tourism
8 A leisure
9 B visitor
10 A traveller

2.7 Tourism Synonyms

1 national
2 (same) day visitor
3 advanced/developed countries
4 inclusive tour
5 domicile
6 alternative/appropriate/green/soft tourism
7 tertiary industries
8 developing/less developed/underdeveloped countries
9 (tour) wholesaler
10 tourism industry

2.8 Tourism Opposites

1 leisure/pleasure/private/holiday (vacation) travel
2 international tourism
3 immigrant
4 individual travel
5 outbound tourism
6 independent tour
7 additional holiday (vacation)
8 (same) day visit
9 tourist destination area
10 rural tourism

2.9 US versus UK Language

1 car hire
2 (motor) car
3 camping site
4 hotel industry
5 (motor) caravan
6 price/rate increase/rise
7 railway
8 holiday
9 holiday/second home
10 holiday trip

2.10 The Language North of the Border

1 glen
2 strath
3 kyle/sound
4 loch
5 Ben
6 Munro
7 mull
8 firth
9 brig
10 bothie/bothy

3 HISTORICAL DEVELOPMENT OF TOURISM

3.1 Worldwide Development

*† 1 Until the early 19th century, the Grand Tour, staying in spas and visiting coastal resorts were, in an embryonic stage, the first manifestations of tourism as we know it today What did they have in common? All three were

A undertaken for health an medicinal reasons ☐
B popular among all age groups ☐
C confined to a small fraction of the population ☐
D in evidence throughout the world ☐

*† 2 An early major effect of the Industrial Revolution was

A increased leisure time of the population ☐
B increased violence ☐
C increased urbanization ☐
C increased conflict in Europe ☐

† 3 The introduction of railways had a major effect on

A decrease in working hours of manual workers ☐
B increase in long-distance stage coach services ☐
C increase in participation in the Grand Tour ☐
D increase in employment ☐

† 4 The original reason for building piers at coastal resorts was

A to break the tidal waves ☐
B to enable steamers to land ☐
C to extend the promenade ☐
D to accommodate entertainment facilities ☐

† 5 American Express was founded to

A assist American visiting Europe ☐
B operate a travel agency business ☐

C supply traveller's cheques ☐
D transport money and valuables ☐

*† 6 The main significance to Thomas Cook's life work lies in
A establishing a retail travel agency business ☐
B guide-book publishing ☐
C introducing the hotel voucher ☐
D originating the inclusive tour ☐

† 7 The Suez Canal was built
A to control the water levels of the Gulf of Suez in relation to the Mediterranean ☐
B to provide water transport between Port Said and Ismailia ☐
C to shorten maritime routes between Europe and the Orient ☐
D for irrigation purposes ☐

*† 8 Railway companies in the 19th century, as well as airlines in the 20th century, built and owned hotels mainly in order to
A diversify their respective businesses ☐
B invest surplus profits ☐
C provide accommodation for crews ☐
D safeguard their passenger traffic ☐

† 9 The main of population migrations on international tourism has been
A a boost to tourism statistics ☐
B increased second home ownership ☐
C increased transport load factors ☐
D a stimulus to visiting friends and relatives ☐

*† 10 The main cause of the decline of deep-sea passenger line shipping after World War II was
A losses of vessels during the war ☐
B diversion of ships to cruising ☐
C growth in air transport ☐
D lack of investment ☐

3.2 British Development I **UK**

1 Most travel in Britain before the 19th century was undertaken for

A. health treatment ☐

B. pilgrimages ☐

C. business and vocational reasons ☐

2 Which was the first major inland resort in Britain?

A Bath ☐

B Buxton ☐

C Harrogate ☐

3 In which century did seaside resorts begin in Britain?

A 17th ☐

B 18th ☐

C 19th ☐

4 Which was the first major seaside resort in Britain?

A Blackpool ☐

B Bournemouth ☐

C Brighton ☐

5 In which century did hotels first appear in Britain?

A 17th ☐

B 18th ☐

C 19th ☐

6 Which decade has been described as the period of 'railway mania' in Britain?

A 1820s ☐

B 1840s ☐

C 1860s ☐

7 Bank Holidays were introduced in Britain in order to

A encourage church attendance on major feast days ☐

B give the banks more time to clear cheques ☐

C ensure a minimum holiday entitlement for all ☐

8 What was the main form of inland passenger public transport in Britain in the early years of the 20th century?

A Bus ☐
B Stage coach ☐
C Train ☐

9 Which period has been described as 'the golden era of bus and coach travel' in Britain?
A 1894-1914 ☐
B 1918-1938 ☐
C 1945-1965 ☐

10 When did the first large holiday camp open in Britain?
A 1936 ☐
B 1946 ☐
C 1956 ☐

3.3 British Development II — UK

1 Arrange the following in chronological order (1, 2, 3) :
A Beginnings of the motor car ....
B First stage coach services ....
C First railway construction ....

2 Arrange the following types of tourism accommodation in the order of their first appearance in Britain (1, 2, 3) :
A Motels ....
B Hotels ....
C Inns ....

3 Thomas Cook scored most of his 'firsts' between 1840 and 1880. Arrange the following in chronological order (1, 2, 3) :
A First round-the-world tour ....
B First hotel coupon issue ....
C First major excursion to London ....

4 Arrange the following events in chronological order (1, 2, 3) :
A The setting up of the Countryside Commission ....
B The passing of the first Town and Country Planning Act ....
C The foundation of the National Trust ....

5 Arrange the following national tourism bodies in the order in which they were established (1, 2, 3) :
A English Tourist Board ....
B Scottish Travel Association ....
C Wales Tourist and Holidays Board ....

6 Three major events brought large numbers of visitors to London within a few years in the late 1940s and early 1950s—in what order (1, 2, 3) :
A Coronation of Queen Elizabeth II ....
B Festival of Britain ....
C Olympic Games ....

7 In what order did the following post-World War II hotels open (1, 2, 3)?
A London Hilton, highest hotel in Britain ....
B Skyway, first major hotel all London Heathrow ....
C Westbury, first new large London hotel ....

8 The first three major hotel cooperative marketing groups were formed in Britain in the 1960s—in what order (1, 2, 3)?
A Inter Hotels ....
B Interchange Hotels ....
C Prestige Hotels ....

9 In what order did the following transport developments occur (1, 2, 3)?
A Opening of the Channel Tunnel ....
B Advanced Passenger Train entry into service ....
C Opening of the first motorway (M1) ....

10 In what order were the following airports opened (1, 2, 3)?
A London City Airport ....
B Gatwick Airport ....
C Stansted Airport as London's 3rd airport ....

3.4 American Development

When

1 was the first railway opened in the USA?
A 1810 ☐
B 1830 ☐
C 1850 ☐

2 was American Express founded?
A 1830 ☐
B 1850 ☐
C 1902 ☐

3 was Yellowstone National Park established?
A 1842 ☐
B 1872 ☐
C 1902 ☐

4 did the first scheduled air service begin in the USA?
A 1905 ☐
B 1915 ☐
C 1925 ☐

5 did the first motels appear in North America?
A 1905 ☐
B 1915 ☐
C 1925 ☐

6 was Hoover Dam built?
A 1920s ☐
B 1930s ☐
C 1940s ☐

7 did Hilton Hotels acquire Statler Hotels?
A 1934 ☐
B 1954 ☐
C 1974 ☐

8 did Disneyland, California, first open?
A 1945 ☐
B 1955 ☐
C 1965 ☐

9 did air transport deregulation begin in the USA?
A 1968 ☐

B 1978 ☐
C 1988 ☐

10 did the North American Free Trade Agreement (NAFTA) come into effect?
A 1974 ☐
B 1984 ☐
C 1994 ☐

3.5 Transport Development

*† **1** When was the world's first passenger railway opened?
A 1830 ☐
B 1840 ☐
C 1850 ☐

*† **2** When did a regular steamship service begin on the North Atlantic?
A 1740 ☐
B 1840 ☐
C 1940 ☐

† **3** When was the Suez Canal opened?
A 1839 ☐
B 1869 ☐
C 1899 ☐

† **4** When did a daily air service begin between London and Paris?
A 1919 ☐
B 1929 ☐
C 1939 ☐

† **5** When was the first commercial air service introduced on the North Atlantic?
A 1929 ☐
B 1939 ☐
C 1949 ☐

† **6** When were economy class air fares introduced on the North Atlantic?

A 1947 ☐
B 1957 ☐
C 1967 ☐

† 7 When were tourist class air fares introduced on the North Atlantic?
A 1945 ☐
B 1952 ☐
C 1959 ☐

*† 8 When did North Atlantic passenger air traffic first exceed sea traffic?
A 1947 ☐
B 1957 ☐
C 1967 ☐

† 9 When was Laker Airways Skytrain launched on the North Atlantic?
A 1967 ☐
B 1977 ☐
C 1987 ☐

† 10 When did Air France and British Airways begin transatlantic Concorde services?
A 1966 ☐
B 1976 ☐
C 1986 ☐

3.6 World Events Since 1945

When did the following events occur?

1 Beginning of the Berlin airlift

....

2 Outbreak of the Korean War

....

3 Hungarian uprising

....

4 Suez crisis

....

5 Six Day War between Egypt and Israel

....

6 Warsaw Pact invasion of Czechoslovakia

....

7 Outbreak of conflict in Northern Ireland

....

8 Falklands War between the UK and Argentina

....

9 Collapse of the Soviet Union

....

10 Gulf War

....

3.7 World Tourism Since 1945

In which year

1 was IATA founded (reconstituted)?

....

2 was the first Bermuda Air Agreement made between the USA and the UK?

....

3 was the European Travel Commission founded?

....

4 were the first jet aircraft services introduced on the North Atlantic?

....

5 did the first United Nations Conference on International Travel and Tourism take place?

....

6 was the International Tourist Year?

....

7 was the World Tourism Organization established?

....

8 was the European Year of Tourism?

....

9 did the annual international tourist arrivals exceed 500 million for the first time?

....

10 was the Eurotunnel officially opened?

....

3.8 Who Was Who in Tourism Worldwide

Who

† 1 was the author of *The Innocents Abroad?*

....

2 pioneered the first regular transatlantic steamship service?

....

† 3 was the best-known 19th century tourist guide publisher?

....

† 4 built the first modern sleeping and dining rail cars?

....

† 5 was the original founder of American Express?

....

† 6 introduced skiing to Switzerland?

....

† **7** was described as 'Hotelkeeper to Kings and King of Hotelkeepers'?

....

† **8** said that there were only three rules for success in the hotel business, location, location, location?

....

† **9** founded the organization which created the world's largest theme parks?

....

† **10** operated the Skytrain on the North Atlantic?

....

3.9 Who Was Who in British Tourism — UK

Who

1 was known as 'Blind Jack of Knaresborough'?

....

2 had a major influence on the grown of seabathing in the 18th century?

....

3 was the first well-known resort publicity officer?

....

4 was described as the 'Father of the Great Western Railway'?

....

5 organized the first inclusive tour abroad?

....

6 was the leading British 19th century tourist guide publisher?

....

7 introduced the Bank Holiday Act in 1871?

....

8 was the author of *Imperial Palace?*

....

9 established the first large-scale holiday camp in Britain?

....

10 produced a report on *The Reshaping of British Railways?*

....

3.10 British Prime Ministers and Tourism **UK**

Which post-war British Prime Minister

1 told the British people that most have never had it so good?

....

2 reduced the foreign currency travel allowance for British residents to nil?

....

3 could see no reason why anyone should wish to take holidays abroad?

....

4 described hotels and catering as 'part of the candyfloss economy'?

....

5 likened service industries to 'taking in each other's washing'?

....

6 had a holiday home in the Scilly Isles?

....

7 was a keen sailor?

....

8 introduced Selective Employment Tax?

....

9 gave the go-ahead for Anglo-French supersonic aircraft?

....

10 removed all exchange controls in the UK?

....

ANSWERS

3.1 Worldwide Development

1 C confined to a small fraction of the population
2 C increased urbanization
3 D increase in employment (directly and indirectly)
4 B to enable steamers to land
5 D to transport money and valuables
6 D originating the inclusive tour
7 C to shorten maritime routes between Europe and the Orient (previously round the Cape of Good Hope)
8 D to safeguard their passenger traffic
9 D stimulus to visiting friends and relatives
10 C growth in air transport

3.2 British Development I

1 C business and vocational reasons
2 A Bath
3 B 18th century
4 C Brighton
5 B 18th century
6 B 1840s (more miles of track opened than during any other decade)
7 C ensure a minimum holiday entitlement for all
8 C Train (with more than one billion passengers per annum)
9 B 1918-1938 (more passengers carried than before or after)
10 A 1936 (by Butlin at Skegness)

3.3 British Development II

1 B 1 First stage coach services (mid-17th century)
C 2 First railway construction (early 19th century)
A 3 Beginnings of the motor car (late 19th century)

2 C 1 Inns (early Middle Ages)
B 2 Hotels (first family hotel in Covent Garden 1774)
A 3 Motels (first Graham Lyon motel at Hythe, Kent, 1953)

3 C 1 First major excursion to London (to Great Exhibition 1851)
B 2 First hotel coupon (1867)
A 3 First round-the-world tour (1872)

4 C 1 National Trust (1895)
B 2 First Town and Country Planning Act (1947)
A 3 Countryside Commission (1968)

5 B 1 Scottish Travel Association (1930)
C 2 Wales Tourist and Holidays Board (1948)
A 3 English Tourist Board (1969)

6 C 1 Olympic Games (1948)
B 2 Festival of Britain (1951)
A 3 Coronation of Queen Elizabeth II (1953)

7 C 1 Westbury (1955)
B 2 Skyway (1960)
A 3 London Hilton (1963)

8 C 1 Prestige Hotels (1966)
B 2 Interchange Hotels (1968)
A 3 Inter Hotels (1969)

9 C 1 First motorway, M1 (1959)
B 2 Advanced Passenger Train (1984)
A 3 Channel Tunnel (1994)

10 B 1 Gatwick Airport (1958)
A 2 London City Airport (1987)
C 3 Stansted Airport (1991)

3.4 American Development

1 B 1830 (the Baltimore & Ohio Railroad, followed by the Boston & Maine Railroad, and then the Charleston & Hamburg (South Carolina) Railroad, all in the same year)

2 B 1850 (by the merger of Wells & Co., founded 1844, Livingston, Fargo & Co., and Wasson & Co., founded 1849)
3 B 1872 (as the first National Park anywhere, by the Yellowstone National Park Act; the Rocky Mountain Parks Act of 1887 established the first Canadian National Park surrounding Banff, Alberta)
4 C 1925 (by Varney Air Lines from Pasco, Washington, to Boise, Idaho and then Elko, Nevada)
5 C 1925 (Vail's Motor Inn at San Luis Obispo, California, is credited as being the first)
6 B 1930s (completed in 1936)
7 B 1954
8 B 1955
9 B 1978 (with the Airline Deregulation Act of that year)
10 C 1994

3.5 Transport Development

1 A 1830 (between Liverpool and Manchester, England)
2 B 1840 (by Cunard)
3 B 1869
4 A 1919 (first by the UK Air Ministry to carry members of the government to the Peace Conference, followed in the same year by two private companies)
5 B 1939 (by Imperial Airways and Pan American)
6 B 1957
7 B 1952
8 B 1957
9 B 1977
10 B 1976

3.6 World Events Since 1945

1 1948
2 1950
3 1956
4 1956
5 1967
6 1968

7 1968
8 1982
9 1991
10 1991

3.7 World Tourism Since 1945

1 1945 (in Havana, Cuba)
2 1946 (renegotiated as Bermuda Two in 1946)
3 1948
4 1958 (by Boeing 101 Paris, New York and Comet London, New York)
5 1963 (in Rome)
6 1967 (designated as such by the United Nations)
7 1975
8 1990 (under the auspices of the European Commission)
9 1992 (when international tourism receipts exceeded US% 100 billion for the first time)
10 1994

3.8 Who Was Who in Tourism Worldwide

1 Mark Twain (1835—1910), US writer, journalist, lecturer
2 Sir Samuel Cunard (1787—1865), shipowner born in Canada, emigrated to England, co-founder of Cunard Line
3 Karl Baedeker (1801—59), German publisher
4 George Mortimer Pullman (1831—97), US inventor, designer, businessman
5 Henry Wells (1805—78), US shipper specializing in valuables and bullion
6 Sir Henry Lunn (1859—1939), British skiing pioneer
7 Cesar Ritz (1850—1918), Swiss-born hotelier
8 Ellsworth Milton Statler (1863—1928), US hotelier
9 Walt Disney (1901—66), US film producer
10 Sir Freddie Laker (1922—), British entrepreneur

3.9 Who Was Who in British Tourism

1 John Metcalf (1717—1810), Scottish engineer and one of the great road-makers of the 18th century

2 Dr. Richard Russell (died 1771), with his treatise on the use of sea water in the treatment of diseases (1752)
3 (Richard) Beau Nash (1674—1762), best known for his brilliant organization of social life at Bath
4 Isambard Kingdom Brunel (1806—59), British engineer who built steam-powered ships, railways and bridges
5 Thomas Cook (1808—92), tour operator, retail travel agent and publisher
6 John Murray (1808—92), famous for his red handbooks
7 Sir John Lubbock (1834—1931), banker, created Baron Avebury 1910
8 Arnold Bennett (1867—1931), whose novel was based on the Savoy Hotel in London
9 William (Billy) Butlin (1899—1980), South African-born, funfair and holiday camp promoter
10 Lord (then Dr. Richard) Beaching (1913—85), known for rationalization of rail services, stations and lines as chairman of British Railways (1962—5)

3.10 British Prime Ministers and Tourism

1 Harold Macmillan (1957-63)
2 Clement Atlee (1945-51)
3 James Callaghan (1976-9)
4 Harold Wilson (1964-6, 1966-70, 1974-6)
5 Edward Heath (1970-4)
6 Harold Wilson (1964-6, 1966-70, 1974-6)
7 Edward Heath (1970-4)
8 Harold Wilson (1964-6, 1966-70, 1974-6)
9 Harold Macmillan (1957-63)
10 Margaret Thatcher (1979-90)

4 GEOGRAPHY OF TOURISM

4.1 Introducing Geography of Tourism

Which two countries share

*† **1** the Iberian Peninsula?

....

*† **2** the Scandinavian Peninsula?

....

What are the main gateways for the following global regions?

† **3** East Africa

....

† **4** South Pacific Islands

....

What are the principal places of pilgrimage for

*† **5** Jews?

....

*† **6** Muslims?

....

How many seasons are there in

† **7** the monsoon region?

....

† **8** the polar region?

....

Who 'gains' a day and who 'loses' a day when crossing the International Date Line?

*† 9 Travellers crossing in the western (Asian) direction

........................a day

*† 10 Travellers crossing in the eastern (American) direction

........................a day

4.2 Country Groupings

What are the collective terms for the following groups of countries?

*† 1 Denmark, Norway, Sweden

....

*† 2 Denmark, Finland, Iceland, Norway, Sweden

....

† 3 Fiji, New Caledonia, Papua New Guinea, Solomon Islands, Vanuatu

....

† 4 Countries of Eastern Europe and former Soviet Union (former planned economies)

....

† 5 Countries of Western Europe, North America, Australia, Japan (market economies)

....

† 6 Countries in the eastern hemisphere

....

† 7 Countries in the western hemisphere

....

*† 8 Countries bordering the Pacific

....

*† 9 Countries bordering the Persian Gulf

....

*† 10 Countries of the New World where Spanish or Portuguese is spoken

....

4.3 World's Coastal Resorts

In which Countries are the following coastal resorts?

*† 1 Acapulco

....

*† 2 Antibes

....

*† 3 Dubrovnik

....

*† 4 Eilat

....

*† 5 Malaga

....

*† 6 Mombasa

....

*† 7 Montego Bay

....

*† 8 Rimini

....

*† 9 Santa Barbara

....

*† 10 Scheveningen

....

4.4 World's Inland Resorts

In which countries are the following inland resorts?

*† **1** Aspen

....

*† **2** Baden-Baden

....

*† **3** Banff

....

*† **4** Chamonix

....

*† **5** Gstaad

....

*† **6** Karlovy Vary (Carlsbad)

....

*† **7** Lillehammer

....

*† **8** Livigno

....

*† **9** Srinagar

....

*† **10** Villach

....

4.5 World's National Parks

In which countries are the following National Parks?

1 Chitwan

....

*† 2 Kakadu

....

3 Komodo

....

*† 4 Mount Cook

....

*† 5 Peak District

....

6 Plitvice Lakes

....

*† 7 Serengeti

....

8 Tikal

....

9 Wood Buffalo

....

*† 10 Yosemite

....

4.6 World's Heritage Attractions

In which Countries are the following heritage attractions?

*† 1 Acropolis

....

*† 2 Brasilia

....

*† 3 Coliseum

....

*† **4** Cordoba mosque

....

*† **5** Great Wall

....

*† **6** Hadrian's Wall

....

*† **7** Mont-St-Michel

....

*† **8** Petra

....

*† **9** Statue of Liberty

....

*† **10** Taj Mahal

....

4.7 Names and By-names of Countries, Regions and Places

What are

† **1** ABC Islands?

....

† **2** ACP States?

....

*† **3** Baltic States?

....

*† **4** Low Countries?

....

*† **5** Nordic Countries?

....

What place is called

† **6** Apple Isle?

....

*† **7** Big Apple?

....

† **8** Big Orange?

....

*† **9** French Canada?

....

† **10** Spice Island?

....

4.8 British Islands and Tourist Regions UK

Identify the following offshore islands :

1 Scenically a microcosm of northern England with archaeological, historical and natural sites, and its own fiscal system

....

2 Scenically a microcosm of southern England with several family resorts and sailing centres

....

3 Around 200 small islands with mild climate, interesting flora and fauna, and unspolit maritime scenery

....

4 A group of islands with attractive climate, coastal scenery and beaches, and a French flavour

....

5 Britain's most northern island group, with a rugged coastline and a unique culture and way of life

....

Identify the **official English tourist board** regions from their main features listed below :

6 The Broads, heritage, the coastline

....

7 The Cotswolds, Shakespeare's country, the Marches

....

8 Hadrian's Wall, Kielder Forest and Water, heritage coast

....

9 A major National Park, lakes and mountains, popular for active recreation

....

10 Two coastlines, two National Parks, many tourist centres

....

4.9 Scales and Instruments

What scale is used for measuring the following :

† **1** Atmospheric pressure?

....

*† **2** Magnitude of earthquakes?

....

† **3** Strength of wind?

....

*† **4** Temperature, with 100 divisions between freezing point and boiling point?

....

*† **5** Temperature, with 180 divisions between freezing point and boiling point?

....

What instrument is used for measuring the following :

† 6 Altitude both in aircraft and on the ground?

....

*† 7 Atmospheric pressure?

....

† 8 Humidity or relative humidity?

....

† 9 Strength and direction of wind?

....

*† 10 Walking distance?

....

4.10 Abbreviations of Countries, Regions and Places

What do the following :

*† 1 BVI

....

*† 2 EU

....

*† 3 FRG

....

*† 4 IOM

....

*† 5 LA

....

*† 6 ME

....

*† 7 NZ

....

*† 8 PNG

....

*† 9 PRC

....

*† 10 WI

....

ANSWERS

4.1 Introducing Geography of Tourism

1 Spain and Portugal
2 Norway and Sweden
3 Nairobi, Kenya
4 Nadi, Fiji
5 Jerusalem
6 Mecca
7 Three (cold, hot, wet)
8 Two (winter and summer)
9 lose
10 gain

4.2 Country Groupings

1 Scandinavia
2 Nordic countries
3 Melanesia
4 Second World
5 First World
6 Old World
7 New World
8 Pacific Rim Countries
9 Gulf States
10 Latin America

4.3 World's Coastal Resorts

1 Mexico
2 France

3 Croatia
4 Israel
5 Spain
6 Kenya
7 Jamaica
8 Italy
9 USA (California)
10 Netherlands

4.4 World's Inland Resorts

1 USA (Colorado)
2 Germany (formerly West Germany)
3 Canada (Alberta)
4 France
5 Switzerland
6 Czech Republic (formerly Czechoslovakia)
7 Norway
8 Italy
9 India
10 Austria

4.5 World's National Parks

1 Nepal
2 Australia
3 Indonesia
4 New Zealand
5 England
6 Croatia
7 Tanzania
8 Guatemala
9 Canada (NW Territories/Alberta)
10 USA (California)

4.6 World's Heritage Attractions

1 Greece
2 Brazil
3 Italy
4 Spain

5 China
6 England
7 France
8 Jordan
9 USA (New Jersey)
10 India

4.7 Names and By-names of Countries, Regions and Places

1 Aruba, Bonaire, Curacao
2 African, Caribbean, Pacific States (under Lome Conventions)
3 Lithuania, Latvia, Estonia
4 Belgium, Holland, Luxembourg
5 Denmark, Finland, Iceland, Norway, Sweden
6 Tasmania, Australia
7 New York, USA
8 California, USA
9 Quebec
10 Zanzibar

4.8 British Islands and Tourist Regions

1 Isle of Man
2 Isle of Wight
3 Scilly Isles
4 Channel Islands
5 Shetland
6 East Anglia
7 Heart of England
8 Northumbria
9 Cumbria
10 West Country

4.9 Scales and Instruments

1 Millibar
2 Richter
3 Beaufort
4 Celsius/centigrade
5 Fahrenheit

6 Altimeter
7 Barometer
8 Hygrometer/wet-bulb thermometer
9 Anemometer (a wind sock gives an indication)
10 Pedometer

4.10 Abbreviations of Countries, Regions and Places

1 British Virgin Islands
2 European Union
3 Federal Republic of Germany
4 Isle of Man
5 Latin America/Los Angeles/Louisiana
6 Maine/Middle East
7 New Zealand
8 Papua New Guinea
9 People's Republic China
10 West Indies/Wisconsin

5 DIMENSIONS OF TOURISM

5.1 Framework of Tourism Statistics

Note : This test may be attempted with or without reference to the following list of terms : inbound, outbound, reimbursed, remunerated, residents, non-residents, three, twelve, tourists, visitors.

Complete the following statements based on *Recommendations on Tourism Statistics* by the World Tourism Organization :

*† **1** Domestic tourism involves...............of a country travelling in the country.

*† **2** Inbound tourism involves...............of a country travelling in the country.

*† **3** Outbound tourism involves............of a country travelling in another country.

† **4** Internal tourism = domestic tourism + ...tourism.

† **5** National tourism = domestic tourism + ... tourism.

† **6** International tourism = inbound tourism + ... tourism.

*† **7** All types of travellers engaged in tourism are described as ....

*† **8** Visitors are sub-divided into...............and same-day visitors.

† **9** The stay in the place visited should not last more than ....months.

† **10** The main purpose of visit should be other then the exercise of an activity................from within the place visited.

5.2 Basic Tourism Statistic

Note : Questions 1-5 may be attempted with or without reference to the following list of terms : average expenditure per day/night, average expenditure per visit, average length of stay, overnight visits, same-day visits, total days/nights, total expenditure, total receipts, total tourist visits, total visits.

Complete the following equations :

*† **1** Total tourist visits + Total .... visits = Total visits

*† **2** Total visits x Average length of stay =...............

Total days/nights = Average length of stay

*† **3**

*† **4** ___________ = Average expenditure per visit

Total visits

Total expenditure = Average expenditure per day/night

*† **5**

Which of the following are **profile** (socio-economic) characteristics and which are **behaviour** (trip) characteristics of tourists?

† **6** Education

....

† **7** Expenditure

....

† **8** Income

....

† **9** Occupation

....

† **10** Purpose of trip

....

5.3 Definitions, Scope and Sources of Tourism Statistics

*† **1** The definition of 'international tourist' recommended by the World Tourism Organization includes *only* visitors who stay in the country visited

A for leisure purposes ☐
B in hotels and similar accommodation ☐
C at least one night ☐
D for less than three months ☐

† **2** Information about the ***actual*** duration of visit by foreign visitors to a country is most reliably obtained from

A accommodation records ☐
B transport records ☐
C a survey of arriving (incoming) visitors ☐
D a survey of departing (returning) visitors ☐

*† **3** The main criterion to be used in the classification of international visitors by place of origin is

A country of birth ☐
B country of issue of passport ☐
C country of nationality ☐
D country of residence ☐

*† **4** For purposes of tourism statistics, 'the means of transport' refers to

A public transport used by a visitor throughout his/her trip ☐
B scheduled transport for which payment is made by the visitor ☐
C transport used by a visitor to travel from his/her place of usual residence to places visited ☐
D local transport used by a visitor at his/her destination ☐

† **5** Which of the following items should be included in 'international tourism expenditure' according to the

recommendations of the World Tourism Organization?

A Bank deposits made during a trip ☐
B Fare payments for international transport ☐
C Cash gifts to relatives during the trip ☐
D Purchases of motor cars ☐

† 6 Estimates of foreign visitors' expenditure in a country are most reliably obtained from

A bank records ☐
B immigration border control ☐
C sample surveys of visitors ☐
D surveys of providers of visitor services ☐

*† 7 Which of the following is generally **true** of outbound tourism statistics of generating countries?

A They measure all outward travel movements. ☐
B They exclude resident aliens. ☐
C They measure numbers of visits, not visitors. ☐
D They include emigrants. ☐

*† 8 Which of the following statements is **false**?

A The number of visits to a destination is the best indication of the value of tourism to the destination. ☐
B Total tourist nights are a better indication of the impact of tourism on a destination than total tourist arrivals. ☐
C Average daily expenditure provides an indication of the quality of tourist traffic to most destinations. ☐
D Average expenditure per visit is a better indication of the quality of tourist traffic to a destination than average length of stay. ☐

† 9 Which of the following forecasting methods drawn on group consensus of expert opinion?

A Delphi ☐
B Extrapolation ☐
C Regression analysis ☐
D Structural modelling ☐

† **10** Link each term in the second column with one abbreviation in the first column to show which international organization first provided what :

1 OECD — A Definition of 'visitor'
2 IMF — B Classification of international payments
3 WTO — C Common framework for national holiday (vacation) surveys

1st column	1	2	3
2nd column			

5.4 Patterns of International Tourism

Note: Questions and answers are based on data published by the World Tourism Organization (WTO) and refer to the mid-1990s.

† **1** In the mid-1990s total international tourist arrivals worldwide were in the range
A 300-400 million ☐
B 400-500 million ☐
C 500-600 million ☐
D 600-700 million ☐

*† 2 What is the main purpose of travel in international tourism?
A Business ☐
B Holiday (vacation) ☐
C Visiting friends and relatives ☐
D Other ☐

*† **3** The main international tourist flows are
A between developed countries ☐
B between developing countries ☐
C from developed to developing countries ☐
D from developing to developed countries ☐

*† **4** Most international tourist movements in the world take place

A across the North Atlantic ☐
B between English-speaking countries ☐
C within the Americas ☐
D within Europe ☐

*† **5** Which global destination region receives most international arrivals and receipts?
A Africa ☐
B Americas ☐
C East Asia & Pacific ☐
D Europe ☐

*† **6** Which is the fastest growing global destination region in international tourism?
A Africa ☐
B Americas ☐
C East Asia & Pacific ☐
D Europe ☐

† **7** Which country receives the highest number of international tourist arrivals?
A France ☐
B Italy ☐
C Spain ☐
D USA ☐

† **8** Which country earns the largest international tourism receipts?
A France ☐
B Italy ☐
C Spain ☐
D USA ☐

† **9** Which country generates the highest number of trips abroad?
A Germany ☐
B Japan ☐
C United kingdom ☐
D USA ☐

† **10** Which country generates the largest expenditure on travel abroad?

A Germany ☐
B Japan ☐
C United Kingdom ☐
D USA ☐

5.5 Tourism-related Surveys in the UK **UK**

Which survey provides information about

1 day trips of British residents in Britain?

....

2 volume and value of overnight trips of UK residents?

....

3 employment and self-employment in British tourism-related industries?

....

4 expenditure of private households in Britain?

....

5 long holidays (vacations, 4 nights or more) of British residents abroad?

....

6 numbers, length of stay and spending of overseas visitors to the UK?

....

7 personal travel patterns of British residents in Britain?

....

8 readership of British newspapers and periodicals?

....

9 short holidays (vacations, 1-3 nights) of UK residents in the UK?

....

10 UK residents' travel abroad for all purposes?

....

5.6 UK Tourism in Figures UK

Note: Questions and answers refer to results of the United Kingdom Tourism Survey (UKTS), which covers **tourism for all purposes by UK residents of one or more nights away from home.** The Survey collects data about both UK and non-UK travel but its main value is in the information it provides about domestic tourism. Questions and answers refer to the mid-1990s.

1 In recent years the annual total number of tourism trips by UK residents in the UK has been in the region of

A 100 milllion + ☐
B 200 million + ☐
C 300 million + ☐

2 The average length of tourism trips by UK residents in the UK has been about

A 4 nights ☐
B 7 nights ☐
C 10 nights ☐

3 The total number of short tourism trips (1-3 nights) has been in comparison with long trips (4 nights or more) each year

A much larger ☐
B much smaller ☐
C about the same ☐

4 Which is the most popular tourism destination region for UK residents within the UK?

A Scotland ☐
B Wales ☐
C West Country ☐

5 What is the main purpose of tourism trips by UK residents in the UK?

A Business ☐
B Holiday (vacation) ☐
C Visiting friends or relatives (VFR) ☐

6 Which part of the UK other than England generates most trips by UK residents in the UK?
A Scotland
B Wales
C Northern Ireland

7 What is the most frequently used method of transport by UK residents to reach their tourism destination in the UK?
A Bus/coach ☐
B Car ☐
C Train ☐

8 What is the most popular type of accommodation used by UK residents on tourism trips in the UK?
A Friends'/relatives' home ☐
B Self-catering accommodation ☐
C Serviced accommodation ☐

9 What is the largest single element of British residents' spending on tourism trips in the UK?
A Accommodation ☐
B Eating out ☐
C Travel ☐

10 Which type of location attracts most tourism spending by UK residents travelling in the UK?
A Countryside ☐
B Towns ☐
C Seaside ☐

5.7 UK in International Tourism UK

Note: Questions and answers refers to results of the International Passenger Survey (IPS), the principal source of statistics of incoming and outgoing travel and tourism to and from the UK; the IPS results are supplemented by estimates of travels between the UK and the Republic of Ireland and of earnings and expenditure for the Channel Island.

1 The total number of visits by overseas residents to the UK in the mid-1990s was

A less than 20 million ☐
B 20-30 million ☐
C more than 30 million ☐

2 Which overseas country generates the largest number of visits to the UK?
A France ☐
B Germany ☐
C USA ☐

3 What is the most frequently used form of transport by overseas visitors to arrive in the UK?
A Air ☐
B Sea ☐
C Channel Tunnel ☐

4 What is the main purpose of visit by overseas residents to the UK?
A Business ☐
B Holiday (vacation) ☐
C Visiting friends or relatives (VFR) ☐

5 What proportion of visits to the UK by overseas residents is on inclusive tours?
A Less than 10% ☐
B 10-20% ☐
C More than 20% ☐

6 The total number of visits abroad by UK residents in the mid-1990s was
A less than 35 million ☐
B 35-45 million ☐
C more than 45 million ☐

7 Which overseas country receives the largest number of visits from UK residents?
A France ☐
B Spain ☐
C USA ☐

8 What is the most frequently used form of transport by UK residents leaving the UK?

A Air ☐
B Sea ☐
C Channel Tunnel ☐

9 What is the main purpose of visits abroad by UK residents?
A Business ☐
B Holiday (vacation) ☐
C Visiting friends or relatives (VFR) ☐

10 What proportion of visits abroad by UK residents is on inclusive tours?
A Less than 30% ☐
B Between 30% and 50% ☐
C More than 50% ☐

5.8 USA in International Tourism

Note: Questions and answers are based on data published by Tourism Industries, an office in the International Trade Administration, US Department of Commerce, and refer to the mid-1990s unless stated otherwise.

1 How many international visitors arrived in the United States each year in the mid-1990s?
A Less than 40 million ☐
B 40-50 million ☐
C More than 50 million ☐

2 Where do most international arrivals to the United States come from?
A Canada ☐
B Mexico ☐
C Overseas ☐

3 Which overseas country generates most international arrivals to the United States?
A Germany ☐
B Japan ☐
C United Kingdom ☐

4 Which South American country generates most international arrivals to the United States

A Argentina ☐
B Brazil ☐
C Venezuela ☐

5 Which is the fastest growing market for international travel to the United States?
A Canada ☐
B Mexico ☐
C Overseas ☐

6 What is the US market share of total international arrivals worldwide?
A Less than 5% ☐
B 5-10% ☐
C More than 10% ☐

7 Which US state receives most international travel receipts?
A California ☐
B Florida ☐
C New York ☐

8 How does the volume of US outbound travel compare with inbound travel to the United States ?
A It is larger ☐
B It is smaller ☐
C It is about the same ☐

9 Which is the main destination for US travel abroad?
A Canada ☐
B Mexico ☐
C Overseas ☐

10 What has been the US travel account balance in the 1990s?
A Positive ☐
B Negative ☐
C Neither (receipts = payments) ☐

5.9 Australia in International Tourism AUS

Note: Questions and answers are based on the *International Visitor Survey*, published annually by the Australian Bureau of Tourism Research.

1 Which is the fastest growing part of Australian tourism?
A Domestic tourism ☐
B Inbound tourism ☐
C Outbound tourism ☐

2 What was the total number of visits to Australia by overseas residents in the mid-1990s?
A Less than 3 million ☐
B 3-4 million ☐
C More than 4 million ☐

3 What was the average length of stay of overseas visitors to Australia in the mid-1990s?
A Less than 20 nights ☐
B 20-30 nights ☐
C More than 30 nights ☐

4 Which global region generates the largest number of visits to Australia?
A Asia ☐
B Europe ☐
C North America ☐

5 Which country generates the largest number of visits to Australia?
A Japan ☐
B New Zealand ☐
C United Kingdom ☐

6 What is the main purpose of visit to Australia by overseas residents?
A Business and professional ☐
B Leisure, recreation and holidays ☐
C Other ☐

7 What is the most frequently used form of transport by visitors arriving in Australia?
A Air ☐
B Sea ☐
C Other ☐

8 What contribution does tourism make to the Australian balance of payments?
A Less than 10 % ☐
B 10-15% ☐
C More than 15% ☐

9 How many trips abroad were made by Australians each year in the mid-1990s?
A Less than 2 million ☐
B 2-3 million ☐
C More than 3 million ☐

10 Between 1985 and 1995 trips abroad by Australians
A increased significantly ☐
B decreased significantly ☐
C remained broadly the same ☐

5.10 The Caribbean in International Tourism **CAR**

Note: Questions and answers are based on the annual *Caribbean Tourism Statistical Report,* published by the Caribbean Tourism Organization.

1 Which Caribbean island country has the largest population?
A Cuba ☐
B Dominican Republic ☐
C Haiti ☐

2 Which Caribbean island country has the largest tourism accommodation capacity?
A Cuba ☐
B Dominican Republic ☐
C Jamaica ☐

3 How many tourists (stayover arrivals) came to the Caribbean in the mid-1990s?
A Less than 10 million ☐
B 10-15 million ☐
C More than 15 million ☐

4 Between 1985 and 1995 international tourist arrivals in the

Caribbean increased in comparison with total world arrivals

A faster ☐
B slower ☐
C at a similar rate ☐

5 Which of the following groups of Caribbean countries received most tourists (stayover arrivals) in the mid-1990s?

A Dutch West Indies ☐
B French West Indies ☐
C US Territories ☐

6 Which Caribbean island country received most tourists (stayover arrivals) in the mid-1990s?

A Dominican Republic ☐
B Jamaica ☐
C Puerto Rico ☐

7 Which was the most important source of tourists (stayover arrivals) to the Caribbean as a whole in the mid- 1990s?

A Caribbean ☐
B Europe ☐
C USA ☐

8 How many cruise passengers arrived in the Caribbean countries in the mid-1990s?

A Around 5 million ☐
B Around 10 million ☐
C Around 15 million ☐

9 Which Caribbean country received most cruise passengers in the mid-1990s?

A Bahamas ☐
B Puerto Rico ☐
C US Virgin Islands ☐

10 Which Caribbean country received most visitor expenditure in the mid-1990s?

A Bahamas ☐
B Dominican Republic ☐
C Puerto Rico ☐

ANSWERS

5.1 Framework to Tourism Statistics

1 residents
2 non-residents
3 residents
4 inbound
5 outbound
6 outbound
7 visitors
8 tourists
9 twelve
10 remunerated

5.2 Basic Tourism Statistics

1 same-day
2 Total days/nights
3 Total visits
4 Total expenditure
5 Total days/nights
6 profile
7 behaviour
8 profile
9 profile
10 behaviour

5.3 Definitions, Scope and Sources of Tourism Statistics

1 C at least one night
2 D a survey of departing (returning) visitors
3 D country of residence
4 C transport used by a visitor to travel from his/her place of usual residence to places visited
5 B Fare payments for international transport
6 C sample surveys of visitors
7 C They measure numbers of visits, not visitors
8 A The number of visits to a destination is *not* the best indication of the value of tourism to the destination.

9 A Delphi

10

1st column	1	2	3
2nd column	C	B	A

5.4 Patterns of International Tourism

1 C 500-600 million (566 million in 1995)
2 B Holiday (vacation) (around 60% of the world total)
3 A between developed countries (around 60% of the world total)
4 D within Europe (around 50% of the world total)
5 D Europe (around 60% of arrivals and 50% of receipts in mid-1990s)
6 C East Asia and Pacific (average 13.5% p.a. arrivals and 16.4% p.a. receipts between 1984 and 1994)
7 A France (60.1 million, Spain 39.3 million, USA 43.4 million, Italy 31.1 million in 1995)
8 D USA (US$ 61.1bn, France US$27.5bn, Italy US$27.5bn, Spain US$25.3bn)
9 D USA (50.8 million in 1995)
10 D USA (US$60.2m in 1995)

5.5 Tourism-Related Surveys in the UK

1 Day Visits Survey (DVS)
2 United Kingdom Tourism Survey (UKTS)
3 Labour Force Survey (LFS)
4 Family Expenditure Survey (FES)
5 British National Travel Survey (BNTS)
6 International Passenger Survey (IPS)
7 National Travel Survey (NTS)
8 National Readership Survey (NRS)
9 United Kingdom Tourism Survey (UKTS)
10 International Passenger Survey (IPS)

5.6 UK Tourism in Figures

1 A 100 million + (121 million in 1995)
2 A 4 nights (1993 : 4.1, 1994 : 3.8, 1995 : 3.7 nights)
3 A much larger (64% compared with 36% in 1995)

4 C West Country (16% trips, 21% nights, 22% spending in 1995)
5 B Holiday (vacation) (55%, VFR 29%, business 12% in 1995)
6 A Scotland (7%, Wales 5%, Northern Ireland 1% of total in 1995)
7 B Car (75%, trips, bus/coach 9%, train 9% in 1995)
8 A Friends'/relatives' home (42% nights, self-catering 26%, serviced 20%in 1995)
9 A Accommodation (1995 survey: 37%, eating out 24%, travel 17%)
10 B Towns (43%, seaside 36%, countryside 21% in 1995)

5.7 UK in International Tourism

1 B 20-30 million (24.0 million in 1995)
2 C USA (1995 : 3.3 million. France 3.2 million, Germany 2.7 million)
3 A Air (1995 : 68%, sea 25%, Channel Tunnel 7%)
4 B Holiday (vacation) (1995 : 44%, business 25%, visiting friends or relatives 19%, miscellaneous 12%)
5 B 10-20% (13.6% in 1995)
6 B 35—45 million (41.9 million in 1995)
7 A France (1995 : 9.7 million, Spain 8.3 million, USA 2.7 million; actually the Irish Republic ranked third, with 28 million in 1995)
8 A Air (1995 : 68%, sea 27%, Channel Tunnel 5%)
9 B Holiday (vacation) (1995 : 67%, business 15%, visiting friends or relatives 12%, miscellaneous 6%)
10 B Between 30% and 50% (36.6% in 1995)

5.8 USA in International Tourism

1 B 40-50 million (43.4 million in 1995)
2 C Overseas (1995 : 47.6%, Canada 33.8%, Mexico 18.6%)
3 B Japan (1995 : 4.6 million, UK 2.9 million, Germany 1.8 million)
4 B Brazil (1995 : 838,000, Venezuela 511,000, Argentina 383,000)

5 C Overseas (+ 12% in 1995, decline from Canada and Mexico)
6 B 5-10% (7.6% in 1995)
7 B Florida (1994 : US$12.0bn, California $11.5bn, New York $7.6bn)
8 A It is larger (*e.g.*, 50.8 million compared to 43.4 million in 1995)
9 C Overseas (1995 : 38%, Mexico 36%, Canada 26%)
10 A Positive throughout the 1990s (*e.g.*, US$19.5bn in 1995)

5.9 Australia in International Tourism

1 B Inbound tourism (between 1985 and 1995 international visitor arrivals increased by an average of 13% p.a., well above the rate of growth of domestic and outbound tourism)
2 B 3-4 million (3.7 million in 1995 but more than 4 million in 1996)
3 B 20-30 nights (21 nights in 1995 and declining)
4 A Asia (51%, Europe 20%, North America 10% in 1995)
5 A Japan (21%, New Zealand 14%, UK 9% in 1995)
6 B Leisure, recreation and holidays (63%, other 22%, business and professional 15% in 1994)
7 A Air (over 99%)
8 B 10-15% (12.7% of current account credits in 1995)
9 B 2-3 million (2.5 million in 1995)
10 A increased significantly (1985 : 1.5 million, 1995 : 2.5 million)

5.10 The Caribbean in International Tourism

1 A Cuba (11.0 million, Dominican Republic 8.0 million, Haiti 7.0 million in 1995)
2 B Dominican Republic (32,000 rooms; Cuba 24,000; Jamaica 21,000 rooms in 1995)
3 B 10-15 million (14.7 in 1995)
4 A Faster (on average 8.4% p.a. compared with 7.2% p.a.)
5 C US Territories (3.6 million, Dutch West Indies 1.4 million, French West Indies 1.1 million in 1995)
6 C Puerto Rico (3.1 million, Dominican Republic 1.9 million, Jamaica 1.1 million in 1995)

7 C USA (over 50%, Europe approx. 20%, Caribbean less than 10 % of the total in 1995)

8 B Around 10 million (9.7 million in 1995)

9 A Bahamas (1.5 million, US Virgin Islands 1.2 million, Puerto Rico 1.0 million in 1995)

10 C Puerto Rico (US$1.8bn, Dominican Republic US$1.6bn, Bahamas US$1.3bn)

6 SIGNIFICANCE OF TOURISM

6.1 Aspects of Tourism

† 1 What has been the main focus of most studies and research in tourism between 1945 and 1995?

A Economic aspect ☐
B Social aspects ☐
C Environmental aspects ☐

† 2 What correlation is there generally between the stage of economic development and the stage of tourism development of a country?

A Positive ☐
B Negative ☐
C None ☐

† 3 Compared with international trade in goods, how much freedom of movement exists between countries in international tourism worldwide?

A It is a relatively free market. ☐
B It is a restricted and regulated market. ☐
C There is not much difference. ☐

*† 4 Which of the following describes the relationship between demand and supply in most tourism markets?

A Stable demand and flexible supply ☐
B Volatile demand and flexible supply ☐
C Volatile demand and fixed supply ☐

† 5 Which of the following market structures is most common in tourism markets with many small operators?

A Perfect competition ☐
B Oligopoly ☐
C Monopolistic competition ☐

*† 6 Which of the following product characteristics applies to most tourist products?

A They are perishable. ☐

B they are stored by travel agents. ☐

C They are transported to customers. ☐

*† 7 Which of the following is likely to show most price-elastic demand?

A Holidays (vacations) ☐

B Pilgrimages ☐

C Visiting friends and relatives ☐

*† 8 Which of the following is likely to show most income-elastic demand ?

A Main holidays ☐

B Additional (secondary) holidays (vacations) ☐

C Convention tourism ☐

*† 9 Which of the following tourist facilities and services are likely to be most labour-intensive?

A Car rental ☐

B Timeshare holiday (vacation) homes ☐

C Travel agencies ☐

† 10 Which of the following tourist attractions, facilities and services can be expected to experience least seasonal variation in their revenues?

A National Parks shops ☐

B Resort condominia ☐

C Suburban travel agencies ☐

6.2 Economic Impacts of Tourism

Note : Question 2 may be attempted with or without reference to the following list : direct, indirect, induced, primary, secondary, leakages, savings.

† 1 A basic change observed in developed economies has been a shift of economic activity from agriculture and manufacturing to services, including tourism. This means that in such an economy invariably

A manufacturing output has been declining
B more people are employed in the tertiary sector
C more foods are imported
D more raw materials are imported

† 2 Complete the following statements about tourism expenditure impacts :
A Tourism expenditure - .... = Direct impact.
B Direct + indirect + ... effects = Total impact.
C ....effects + induced effects = Secondary effects.
D Total impact -..........effects = Direct impact.

*† 3 Which of the following are normally direct (D) and which are indirect (I) recipients of tourism expenditure?
A Building firms ....
B Laundries ....
C Railways ....
D Travel agents ....

*† 4 Rank the following (1, 2, 3, 4) located in a resort area according to the likely dependence on tourism for their business :
A Banks ....
B Public utilities ....
C Souvenir shops ....
D Taxis ....

† 5 Which of the following ratios is the main single indication of the relative importance of tourism in an economy?
A Foreign exchange earnings to total exports ☐
B Foreign exchange earnings to exports of services ☐
C Tourism spending to GDP or GNP ☐
D Tourism spending to total consumer spending ☐

*† 6 Which of the following are Debits (Dr) and which are Credits (Cr) in a country's balance of payments?
A Spending by foreign tourists in the country ....
B Fares paid by residents to foreign airlines ....
C Remittances from nationals working abroad ....
D Tourism capital investment in another country ....

*† 7 Which of the following factors is conducive to high *net* foreign currency earnings from tourism?
A High expatriate labour □
B High foreign investment □
C High indigenous ownership of tourism industry □
D High propensity to import □

† 8 Which of the following statements about tourism income multipliers is true?
A As long as demand exists for locally produced goods and services, each successive round of spending generates new income. □
B Simple 'ad hoc' models yield more accurate results than those calculated with input-output analysis. □
C Regions of a country tend to experience higher multiplier values than countries. □
D The main value of tourism multipliers is for long-term rather than short-term planning. □

† 9 Which of the following is conducive to low income multiplier values in tourism?
A Low diversification of the economy □
B Low level of imports □
C Low propensity to save □
D Low taxation □

*† **10** If the employment multiplier of a destination with direct tourism employment of 1,000 people is 1.25, what is the total tourism-related employment? ....

6.3 Social Aspects and Impacts of Tourism

1 Which of the following groups of local residents has been found in research studies to be most favourably disposed to tourism development?
A Academics □
B Businessmen □
C Local government officers □
D Police □

† 2 The process and the results of interaction between different cultures is described in sociological terms as
A acclimatization ☐
B acculturation ☐
C familiarization ☐
D naturalization ☐

† 3 The belief that the attitudes and behaviour of one's own ethnic group are superior to those of others, is known in sociological terms as
A anthropomorphism ☐
B cultural relativism ☐
C ethnicism ☐
D ethnocentrism ☐

† 4 The tendency for an individual or a group to imitate the behaviour of another and to assimilate it as one's own is known in sociological terms as
A accommodation ☐
B assimilation ☐
C demonstration effect ☐
D replication ☐

† 5 The contempt dislike or fear of strangers or foreigners or of strange or foreign places is called
A agoraphobia ☐
B alienation ☐
C claustrophobia ☐
D xenophobia ☐

6 Arrange in chronological order (1, 2, 3, 4) the following stages proposed by American sociologist G.V. Doxey (1976) as a framework for assessing the social impacts of tourism in a destination :
A antagonism ....
B apathy ....
C euphoria ....
D irritation ....

† 7 The term 'social tourism' describes
- A tourism to socialist countries ☐
- B travel for educational purposes ☐
- C tourism which fosters group activities ☐
- D assisted holidays (vacations) for disadvantaged groups in society ☐

8 Which of the following has been found endemic to tourism in research studies?
- A Alcoholism ☐
- B Gambling ☐
- C Prostitution ☐
- D None of the above ☐

9 Which of the following statements is true?
- A Tourism is devoid of cultural enrichment. ☐
- B Tourism can be a lever for social change. ☐
- C Tourism is the only form of exposure of societies to different cultures. ☐
- D Unlike the hosts, tourists are not influenced in their own attitudes and habits by tourism. ☐

10 Is there any evidence for the following statements?
- A Tourism is the opium of mankind.
  (L. Turner and J. Ash, 1975) YES/NO
- B Tourism is a secular substitute for organized religion.
  (D. MacCannell, 1976) YES/NO
- C Holidays abroad can damage your health.
  (P. Rivers, 1972) YES/NO
- D Tourism is a passport to development.
  (E. de Kadt, 1979) YES/NO

6.4 Environmental Aspects and Impacts of Tourism

† 1 Link each aspect of the environment in the first column with the part of the world in the second column where it is of particular concern :

1 coral reefs	A Amazonia
2 destruction of forests	B Mediterranean
3 water quality	C Africa
4 wildlife	D Pacific Ocean

Aspect of the environment	1	2	3	4
Part of world				

*† 2 Link each type of pollution in the first column with the main cause shown in the second column :

1 air pollution — A aircraft
2 noise pollution — B motor car
3 land pollution — C sewage discharge into the sea
4 water pollution — D dumping of waste

Type of pollution	1	2	3	4
Main cause				

*† 3 Link each problem in the first column with the type of location where it is prominent in the second column :

1 erosion and landslides — A inland resorts
2 oil from motor boats — B coastal resorts
3 traffic congestion — C mountains
4 infrastructure overload — D inland waters

Problem	1	2	3	4
Type of location				

† 4 Link each environmental issue in the first column with one of the effects in the second column :

1 acid rain — A higher fuel prices
2 global warming — B risk of skin cancer
3 fossil fuels depletion — C damage to monuments
4 ozone layer depletion — D increase in sea levels

Issue	1	2	3	4
Effect				

† 5 Give a synonym for each of the following terms :

A green audit

....

B green tourism

....

C greenhouse effect

....

D inexhaustible resources

....

† 6 Link each explanation in the first column with the term to which it applies in the second column :

1 Maintaining something in its present form	A Renovation
2 Protecting from decay and destruction	B Restoration
3 Restoring something to good condition	C Preservation
4 Returning something to previous condition	D Conservation

Explanation	1	2	3	4
Term				

† 7 What are the following types and forms of tourism called?

A Forms of tourism which seek to avoid adverse and enhance positive impacts

....

B Type and scale of tourism considered suitable in view of area conditions

....

C Ecologically sustainable trips and visits which pro mote conservation

....

D Holidays (vacations) in the countryside working to improve the environment

....

† 8 Assuming typical passenger numbers and load factors, which of the following means of transport uses least fuel per passenger mile?

A Coach ☐
B Jumbo jet ☐
C Medium car ☐
D Train ☐

*† 9 Which of the following recreational activities is least detrimental to the environment?

A Motorcycling ☐
B Snowmobiling ☐
C Water skiing ☐
D Hang gliding ☐

† 10 What are the following awards called?

A European award to destinations with most innovative and effective tourism environmental policies

....

B European award for beaches meeting strict water quality standards

....

6.5 Measures of Tourism Distribution and Impacts

What are the following measures called?

1 Ratio of visitors to residents in an area

....

2 Ratio of tourist beds to resident population of an area

....

3 Ratio of incoming to outgoing tourist flows in an area

....

4 Ratio of nights spent in an area from particular areas of origin

....

5 Ratio of nights spent at a destination to total nights on a trip

....

6 Measure of internal accessibility of a region based on established routes

....

7 Measure of relative compactness and internal accessibility of a region

....

8 Measure of the travel patterns of an origin in relation to destinations

....

9 Measure summarizing data on temporal use levels

....

10 Measure of tourism potential of different regions

....

6.6 Developed Countries and Tourism

Note: Questions and Answers 6-9 refer to OECD member countries and are based on data published in the 1995 edition *Tourism Policy and International Tourism in OECD Member Countries.* OCED covers twenty-nine mainly developed countries in Europe, North America, Australia and Japan.

† **1** Who postulated that societies passed through five stages of economic development from the traditional society to maturity?

A John Kenneth Galbraith ☐
B Walt Whitman Rostow ☐
C Adam Smith ☐

*† **2** Which of the following is the most commonly used indicator of standard of living in cross-country comparisons?

A Gross national product (GNP) per capita ☐
B Holiday (vacation) propensity of population ☐
C Number of cars per 1,000 population ☐

*† **3** Which of the following characteristics applies to most developed countries?
A Export trade dominated by raw materials ☐
B Fast rate of population growth ☐
C Large tertiary sector ☐

*† **4** Which of the following statements about developed countries is **false**?
A They have high holiday (vacation) propensities. ☐
B They are (not) important tourist destinations. ☐
C They are major tourism generators. ☐

† **5** In which of the following countries has tourism contributed to overall economic development so as to raise it from developing to developed country status in the second half of the 20th century?
A Bahamas ☐
B Cyprus ☐
C Spain ☐

6 What is the approximate ratio of international tourism receipts to the gross domestic product (GDP) in developed countries as a whole?
A Around 1% ☐
B Around 3% ☐
C Around 5% ☐

7 What is the approximate ratio of international tourism expenditure to the private final consumption (PFC) in developed countries as a whole?
A Around 1% ☐
B Around 2% ☐
C Around 3% ☐

8 What is the approximate share of international tourism receipts in exports of goods and services in developed countries as a whole?

A Around 5% ☐
B Around 10% ☐
C Around 15% ☐

9 What is the approximate share of international tourism expenditure in imports of goods and services in developed countries as a whole?
A Around 5% ☐
B Around 10% ☐
C Around 15% ☐

10 What proportion of world trade in good and services is approximately accounted for by international tourism?
A Around 7% ☐
B Around 10% ☐
C Around 15% ☐

6.7 Developing Countries and Tourism

1 Which of the following Commissions has been particularly concerned with developing countries?
A Brandt Commission ☐
B Brundtland Commission ☐
C Outdoor Recreation Resources Review Commission ☐

*† 2 Which of the following characteristics applies to most developing countries?
A They are short of land. ☐
B They are short of labour. ☐
C They are short of capital. ☐

*† 3 Which of the following statements if **false**?
A Most developing countries are in Africa, Asia or Latin America. ☐
B Many developing countries are island economies. ☐
C Most developing countries generate more tourism than they receive. ☐

† **4** Which of the following is **not** considered to be a developing country?

A Brazil ☐
B Israel ☐
C Panama ☐

*† **5** The main reason why tourism is an attractive development option for many developing countries is because it
A is a 'clean' industry ☐
B earns foreign currency ☐
C smooth out seasonal fluctuations in exports ☐

6 What has been the rate of growth of international tourist arrivals in developing countries as a whole compared with developed countries as a whole in the 1990s?
A Slower ☐
B Faster ☐
C About the same ☐

7 What approximate share of total international tourism (arrivals and receipts) has accrued to developing countries in the 1990s?
A One-fifth ☐
B One-quarter ☐
C One-third ☐

8 How do tourism multiplier values in developing countries normally compare with those in developed countries?
A They are higher. ☐
B They are lower. ☐
C They are about the same. ☐

9 Which of the following developing countries receives most international tourist arrivals?
A Mexico ☐
B Singapore ☐
C Thailand ☐

10 Which of the following developing countries earns most from international tourism?
A Mexico ☐

B Singapore ☐
C Thailand ☐

6.8 Tourism and the UK Economy UK

1 What is the approximate ratio of total tourism spending (see note 1) to the UK gross domestic product (DGP)
A Around 2% ☐
B Around 4% ☐
C Around 8% ☐

2 What is the approximate ratio of foreign exchange earnings from tourism (see note 2) to total UK exports?
A Around 3% ☐
B Around 5% ☐
C Around 10% ☐

3 What is the approximate ratio of foreign exchange earnings from tourism (see note 2) to total UK exports of services?
A Around 20% ☐
B Around 30% ☐
C Around 40% ☐

4 What is the approximate ratio of total tourism spending (see note 1) to total UK consumer spending?
A Around 3% ☐
B Around 6% ☐
C Around 10% ☐

5 Which of the following industries generates highest export earnings?
A Petroleum products ☐
B Textiles ☐
C Tourism (see note 2) ☐

6 Which of the following economic activities receives most of overseas visitors' spending (see note 3) in the UK?
A Hotels and other accommodation ☐
B Retailing ☐
C Transport ☐

7 Which of the following economic activities receives most of domestic tourism spending (see note 4) in the UK?
A Hotels and other accommodation ☐
B Catering ☐
C Transport ☐

8 Which of the following economic activities receives most of UK residents' spending on day trips?
A Catering ☐
B Retailing ☐
C Transport ☐

9 How many people are estimated to be directly and indirectly employed in the UK due to tourism?
A Around 0.5 million ☐
B Around 1 million ☐
C Around 1.5 million ☐

10 Every direct job in UK tourism is estimated to give rise to how much employment elsewhere in the economy?
A Another half-a-job ☐
B Another job ☐
C Two other jobs ☐

Notes : [1] Including visitors to the UK and their fare payments of UK carriers plus domestic tourism, excluding day trips.
[2] Including fare payments to UK carriers.
[3] Excluding fare payments to UK carriers.
[4] Excluding day trips.

6.9 Tourism and the US Economy **US**

Note : Questions and Answers are based on Economic *Review of Travel in America* published by the Travel Industry Association of America. Travel and tourism spending denotes the sum of domestic and foreign visitor expenditures in the USA. In Question 2 'foreign exchange earnings' include international travel and transport receipts.

1 What is the approximate ratio of total travel and tourism spending to the US Gross National Product (GNP)?
A Around 3% ☐
B Around 6% ☐
C Around 10% ☐

2 What is the approximate ratio of foreign exchange earnings from travel and tourism to total US exports?
A Around 3% ☐
B Around 5% ☐
C Around 10% ☐

3 Which of the following US travel-related industries has the highest sales?
A Air transport ☐
B Food service ☐
C Lodging ☐

4 Rank the following US industries according to their receipts (1, 2, 3) :
A Automotive dealers ....
B Food stores ....
C Travel and tourism ....

5 How large is the sales multiplier of travel and tourism spending in the USA?
A Less than 2 ☐
B Between 2 and 3 ☐
C More than 3 ☐

6 Approximately how many jobs are supported directly by travel and tourism spending in the USA?
A Less than 6 million ☐
B Between 6 and 8 million ☐
C More than 8 million ☐

7 What approximate proportion of total US non-agricultural payroll employment is directly due to travel and tourism?
A Around 5% ☐
B Around 10% ☐
C Around 15% ☐

8 How much do wages and salaries generated directly by travel and tourism spending in the USA increase as a result of the multiplier process?

A Less than 2 times ☐

B 2-3 times ☐

C More than 3 times ☐

9 What approximate proportion of the combined tax revenue of US federal, state and local governments is contributed as a result of travel and tourism spending?

A 2-3% ☐

B 3-4% ☐

C 4-5% ☐

10 Which of the following US Census regions earns most from combined US and foreign visitor spending?

A New England ☐

B Pacific ☐

C South Atlantic ☐

6.10 International Organizations

Below are listed abbreviations of names of international organizations concerned with economic, social and environmental aspects of tourism. What do they stand for?

† **1** ASEAN

....

*† **2** ILO

....

*† **3** OECD

....

† **4** TEN

....

† **5** UNCTAD

....

*† **6** UNDP

....

† **7** UNEP

....

*† **8** UNESCO

....

*† **9** WTO

....

† **10** WTTC

....

ANSWERS

6.1 Economic Aspects of Tourism

1 A Economic aspects
2 C None
3 A It is a relatively free market.
4 C Volatile demand and fixed supply
5 C Monopolistic competition
6 A They are perishable
7 A Holidays (vacations)
8 B Additional (secondary) holidays (vacations)
9 C Travel agencies
10 B Resort condominia (they are normally owned—interior units individually, land and buildings in common)

6.2 Economic Impacts of Tourism

1 B more people are employed in the tertiary sector
2 A Leakages
B Induced
C Indirect
-D Secondary
3 A Indirect
B Indirect
C Direct

D Direct
4 C 1 Souvenir shops
D 2 Taxis
A 3 Banks
B 4 Public utilities
5 C Tourism spending to GDP or GNP
6 A Credits
B Debits
C Credits
D Debits
7 C High indigenous ownership of tourism industry
8 A As long as demand exists for locally produced goods and services, each successive round of spending generates new income
9 A Low diversification of the economy
10 1,250

6.3 Social Aspects and Impacts of Tourism

1 B Businessmen
2 B acculturation (also described as accommodation/ assimilation)
3 D ethnocentrism
4 C demonstration effect
5 D xenophobia
6 C 1 euphoria
B 2 apathy
D 3 irritation
A 4 antagonism
(In *Heritage Canada,* Vol. 2, 1976, pp. 26-7)
7 D assisted holidays (vacations) for disadvantaged groups in society
8 D None of these
9 B Tourism can be a lever for social change
10 A No (*The Golden Hordes,* London: Constable)
B No (*The Tourist,* London: Macmillan)
C Yes (*The Restless Generation,* London : Davis-Poynter)
D Yes (*Tourism-Passport to Development?* Oxford : OUP)

6.4 Environmental Aspects and Impacts of Tourism

1

Aspect of environment	1	2	3	4
Part of world	D	A	B	C

2

Type of pollution	1	2	3	4
Main cause	B	A	D	C

1	2
A	B

Also acceptable

3

Problem	1	2	3	4
Type of location	C	D	A	B

4

Issue	1	2	3	4
Effect	C	D	A	B

5 A environmental audit
B alternative/appropriate/responsible/soft tourism
C global warming
D renewable resources

6

Explanation	1	2	3	4
Term	C	D	A	B

7 A Alternative/appropriate/green/responsible/soft tourism
B Appropriate/responsible tourism
C Ecotourism/green tourism
D Green holidays (vacation)

8 A Coach (0.023lb per passenger mile, train 0.073lb, medium car 0.180lb, jumbo jet 0.347lb, *Aeronautical Journal,* Vol. 78, No, 765, 1974)

9 D Hang gliding

10 A European Prize for Tourism and the Environment
B Blue Flag

6.5 Measures of Tourism Distribution and Impacts

1 Tourist intensity index (D.E. Lundberg, 1974)
2 Tourist function index (P. Defert, 1967)

3 Ratio index (M. Jensen-Verbeke, 1995)
4 Concentration index (M. Jensen-Verbeke, 1995)
5 Trip index (D.G. Pearce and J.M. Elliott, 1995)
6 Connectivity index (S.L.J. Smith, 1989)
7 Compactness index (W.J. Coffey, 1981)
8 Directional bias index (R.I. Wolfe, 1966)
9 Peaking index (D.J. Stynes, 1978)
10 Tourism attractiveness index (G.E. Gearing, W.W. Swart and T. Var, 1974)

See the following sources for details :

Q1 Lundberg, D.E. (1974) *The Tourist Business,* 2nd edn, Boston, MA : Cahners.
Q2 Smith, S.L.J. (1989) *Tourism Analysis : A Handbook,* London : Longman.
Q3,4 *Tourism Management,* Vol. 16, No. 1, February 1995.
Q 5 *Journal of Travel Research,* Vol. 32, No. 1, 1995 : 6-9.
Q 6-10 Smith, S.L.J. (1989), as above.

6.6 Developed Countries and Tourism

1 B Walt Whitman Rostow (1959), US economic historian (1916-)
2 A Gross national product (GNP) per capita
3 C Large tertiary sector
4 B They are not important tourist destinations.
5 C Spain
6 A Around 1%
7 B Around 2%
8 A Around 5%
9 A Around 5%
10 A Around 7%

6.7 Developing Countries and Tourism

1 A Brandt Commission (Independent Commission on International Development Issues set up in 1977 at the suggestion of the President of the World Bank under the Chairmanship of Willy Brandt, German statesman and Nobel Peace Prize winner in 1971)

2 C They are short of capital
3 C Most developing countries (do not) generate more tourism than they receive
4 B Israel
5 B earns foreign currency
6 B Faster
7 B One-quarter
8 B They are lower
9 A Mexico (1995 : 20.0m, Singapore 6.6m, Thailand 6.5m)
10 B Singaporę (1995 : US$ 7,550m, Thailand US$ 6,617m, Mexico US$ 6,070m.

6.8 Tourism and the UK Economy

1 B Around 4% : 1993 : 3.8%, 1994 : 3.8%, 1995 : 4.0%
2 B Around 5% : 1993 : 4.6%, 1994 : 4.8%, 1995 : 5.1% (Provisional)
3 B Around 30% : 1993 : 30.4%, 1994 : 30.1%, 1995 : 33.4% (Provisional)
4 B Around 6% : 1993 : 6.0%, 1994 : 6.0%, 1995 : 6.2% (Provisional)
5 C Tourism (1995 : £12.1m, petroleum products £8.7m, textiles £3.3m)
6 A Hotels and other accommodation (1992 survey : 36.1%, retailing 24.5%, travel within UK 8.0%)
7 A Hotels and other accommodation (1995 survey : 37.0%, eating out 24.0%, travel within UK 17.0%)
8 A Catering (1992 survey : meals, snacks, alcoholic and non-alcoholic drinks 38%; gifts, souvenirs, clothes 22%; fuel, fares, parking charges 18%)
9 C Around 1.5 million
10 A Another half-a-job

6.9 Tourism and the US Economy

1 B Around 6%
2 C Around 10%
3 B Food service
4A 1 Automotive dealers
B 2 Food stores

C 3 Travel and tourism
5 B Between 2 and 3 (2.4)
6 B Between 6 and 8 million (6.6 million in 1995)
7 A Around 5%
8 B 2-3 times (2.4 times including indirect and induced effects)
9 C 4-5% (4.3% in 1995)
10 C South Atlantic

6.10 International Organizations

1 Association of South East Asian Nations
2 International Labour Organisation
3 Organization for Economic Cooperation and Development
4 Third World European Ecumenical Network
5 United Nations Conference on Trade and Development
6 United Nations Development Programme
7 United Nations Environmental Programme
8 United Nations Educational, Scientific and Cultural Organization
9 World Tourism Organization
10 World Travel and Tourism Council

7 THE TOURISM INDUSTRY

7.1 Tourism as an Industry

Note : Question 5 may be attempted with or without reference to the following list : activities, industries, products, services, domestic, foreign .

*† **1** Strictly speaking, what makes up an industry?

A Establishments ☐
B Firms ☐
C Occupations ☐

† **2** What is the principal purpose of a Standard Industrial Classification?

A To provide a basis for business taxation ☐
B To serve as a framework for industry associations ☐
C To promote uniformity and comparability of official statistics ☐

*† **3** Which of the following statements is **true** of the tourism industry?

A It is synonymous with leisure industry. ☐
B It is synonymous with hospitality industry. ☐
C It is synonymous with tourism supply. ☐

*† **4** Which of the following statements about tourism industries is **false**?

A The tourism industry may be defined by reference to the market. ☐
B Most industries serving tourists are service industries. ☐
C Tourism-related industries serve only tourists. ☐

*† **5** Insert the missing words in the following definition of the tourism industry by the United Nations Conference on Trade and Development (1971) :

....the tourist sector or the tourism industry . . . can be broadly conceived as representing the sum of those industrial and commercial

A...............................producing goods and

B...............................wholly or mainly consumed by

C...............................visitors or domestic tourists.

*† **6** Which of the following activities forms part of the tourism industry?

A Hotel construction ☐

B Conference center ownership and management ☐

C Food manufacturing ☐

*† **7** Which of the following characteristics is common to all or most of the tourism industry?

A High labour productivity ☐

B Low seasonality ☐

C Product perishability ☐

*† **8** Which of the following activities usually accounts for the largest proportion of tourism industry employment?

A Hotels and catering ☐

B Passenger transportation ☐

C Tour operations and travel agencies ☐

† **9** Diversification of firms takes place

A mainly from tourism into other industries ☐

B mainly from other industries into the tourism industry ☐

C equally in both directions ☐

† **10** What forms of integration are illustrated by the following?

A Meger of two hotel companies

....

B Acquisition of a wine-shipping firm by a restaurant company

....

C Acquisition of a travel agency chain by a tour operator

....

7.2 Visitor Attraction Worldwide

Note : Question I may be attempted with or without reference to the following list : choice, environment, industry, motivation, preference, purchases.

† **1** Insert the missing words in the following definition of (managed) visitor attraction by British author V.T.C. Middleton (1994) :

......elements within the A................ that largely determine consumers' B.................and influence prospective buyers' C.................

† **2** Which of the following describes best the visitor attraction product?

A The resources offered to the visitor ☐
B What is the visitor buys ☐
C The visitor experience ☐

† **3** Which of the following factors is most important in determining the size of the market for a visitor attraction?

A Availability of refreshments and shopping ☐
B Distance from concentrations of population ☐
C Variety of activities on offer ☐

*† **4** Which of the following are motivators (M) and which are determinants (D) of visits to attractions?

A Atmosphere ....
B Enjoyment ....
C Leisure time ....

† **5** What are the generic terms for the following groups of man-made visitor attractions?

A Castles, palaces, cathedrals, churches

....

B Protected ancient sites, such as fortifications and burial mounds

....

C Sites and structures identified with mining, industrial processes and past transportation

....

*† 6 Which of the following represents the main source of revenue in most private sector visitor attractions?

A Admission charges ☐
B Meals and refreshments ☐
C Retailing ☐

*† 7 Which of the following is commonly the largest element of operating costs of large new private sector visitor attractions?

A Maintenance ☐
B Payroll ☐
C Promotion ☐

† 8 Complete the following equations, the first a common measure of performance in private sector, the second in public and voluntary sector visitor attractions :

A Total visitor expenditure
= Visitor spending per head

$$B \quad \frac{\rule{6cm}{0.4pt}}{\text{Operating expenditure}} = \text{Recovery rate}$$

† 9 Which of the following places are best known for their site attractions and which for their event attractions?

A Luxor, Egypt ....
B Oberammergau, Germany ....
C Orlando, USA ....

† 10 Which of the following US visitor attractions have regional (R), national (N) or international (I) catchment areas?

A Colonial Williamsburg, Virginia ....
B Disneyworld, Florida ....
C Mt Charleston, Nevada ....

7.3 Visitor Attractions in Britain **UK**

Which of the following organization operates visitor attractions in the public sector (P) and which in the voluntary sector (V)?

1 English Heritage ....

2 The National Trust ....

Which of the following visitor attractions has a regional (R) and which has a national (N) catchment area?

3 Blackpool Pleasure Beach ....

4 Alton Towers, Staffordshire ....

What method of on-site transport is used at the following visitor attractions?

5 Jorvik Viking Museum, York ....

6 Wigan Pier, Greater Manchester ....

Which is the largest and which is the smallest National Park in England?

7 The largest ....

8 The smallest ....

What UNESCO World Heritage Site is in

9 Scotland? ....

10 Wales? ....

7.4 Transport Modes

Which transport mode offers most prominently the following advantages to tourists over other modes?

*† 1 Sightseeing for groups ....

*† 2 Transporting luggage from door to door ....

In which country is a motorway known as an

*† 3 autobahn? ....

*† 4 autostrada? ....

In which country are to be found the following high-speed trains?

† 5 Bullet Train ....

† 6 Train a Grande Vitesse (TGV) ....

What are the following vessels called?

† 7 A twin-hull boat or ship designed to cut through the waves ....

† 8 A vessel moving above the water surface on retractable submerged fins or foils ....

What form of transport do most foreign tourists use to arrive in

† 9 Canada? ....

*† 10 United Kingdom? ....

7.5 Air Transport

*† 1 Which of the following characteristics applies to air transport?
- A High labour intensiveness ☐
- B Low capital intensiveness ☐
- C High fixed costs ☐

† 2 Which of the following data are used to calculate the revenue load factor?
- A Gross registered tonnage and passenger capacity ☐
- B Load tonne-kilometers and capacity tonne-kilometers ☐
- C Passenger kilometers and seat kilometers ☐

*† 3 Which of the following is described as a transit passenger?

A One scheduled to travel on the same vehicle to its final destination ☐
B One who changes vehicle to continue a journey by a connecting service ☐
C One who breaks a journey at an intermediate point ☐

*† 4 Which of the following statements is true worldwide?

A More people fly on international routes than on domestic routes ☐
B Charter flights have higher load factors than scheduled flights ☐
C More charter flights are domestic than international ☐

*† 5 Which of the following codes used by airlines and others in reservations, time-tables and ticketing consists of three letters?

A Codes denoting airlines ☐
B Codes denoting cities/airports ☐
C Codes denoting countries/states ☐

† 6 What is the equivalent in air transport of the Athens Convention (1974) which limits the liability of shipping companies?

A Berne Convention ☐
B Chicago Convention ☐
C Warsaw Convention ☐

† 7 Which of the following so-called freedoms of the air covers most international point-to-point traffic?

A Cabotage rights ☐
B Technical rights ☐
C Traffic rights ☐

† 8 Which of the following is a cabotage route?

A Los Angeles –Honolulu ☐
B Prague-Bratislava ☐
C Sydney –Wellington ☐

*† 9 The main cause of the decline in transatlantic sea transport after World War II was
- A decline in bulk freight ☐
- B decrease in European migration to North America ☐
- C growth in air transport ☐

† 10 British Airways was formed by the merger of
- A British European Airways and British Caledonian ☐
- B British European Airways and Imperial Airways ☐
- C British European Airways and British Overseas Airways Corporation ☐

7.6 Transport Synonyms and Opposites

Give a synonym for each of the following transport terms :

† 1 back load

....

*† 2 carry-on-baggage

....

*† 3 layover

....

† 4 Plimsoll line

....

*† 5 stern

....

Give an opposite of each of the following transport teams :

*† 6 aft

....

*† 7 charter airline

....

*† 8 starboard

....

*† 9 surface transport

....

† 10 transfer passenger

....

7.7 Hotels and Other Tourism Accommodation

† 1 Which of the following characteristic applies to hotels?
A Low capital to revenue ratio ☐
B Low ratio of fixed to variable costs ☐
C High investment intensity ☐

† 2 What terms describe the following relationships in hotels?
A Bed capacity sold and available bed capacity

....

B Room capacity sold and available room capacity

....

C Room sales and the number of rooms sold

....

*† 3 What is normally the largest element of capital investment in most hotels in developing countries?
A Land ☐
B Building ☐
C Interior assets ☐

*† 4 What is normally the largest single element of hotel operating costs in developed countries?
A Consumables ☐
B Overheads ☐
C Payroll ☐

*† **5** Which of the following statements about hotel accommodation is **true**?

A Hotel room occupancies are normally higher than bed occupancies. ☐

B Capital cities tend to have lower annual hotel occupancies than coastal resorts. ☐

C Business centres have normally higher occupancies at weekends than midweek. ☐

*† **6** Which of the following statements about tourism accommodation is **false**?

A It determines destination capacity for overnight visitors. ☐

B It determines most tourists' choice of destinations. ☐

C It influences the choice of destinations by tour operators. ☐

*† 7 Rank the following tourism accommodation in order of labour intensiveness in operation (1, 2, 3) :

A Motels ☐

B Camping sites ☐

C Hotels ☐

*† 8 Categorization of hotel accommodation by type and range of facilities and services is called

A hotel registration ☐

B hotel classification ☐

C hotel grading ☐

*† 9 Link each type of tourism accommodation in the first column with one most likely group of users in the second column :

1 farms — A students

2 hotels — B families with children

3 youth hostels — C package tours

Accommodation	1	2	3
Users			

† 10 What is the world's largest hotel franchise system?

A Best Western International ☐

B Holiday Inn Worldwide ☐

C Hospitality Franchise Systems ☐

7.8 Accommodation Types and Tariffs

In which country is to be found

† **1** a bach?

....

† **2** a gite?

....

† **3** a parador?

....

† **4** a pousada?

....

† **5** a ryokan?

....

What is the American term for the hotel tariff which includes

† **6** room only and no meals?

....

† **7** room and Continental breakfast?

....

† **8** room and English breakfast?

....

† **9** room, breakfast and one main meal?

....

† **10** room and three meals per day?

....

7.9 Tour Operations and Travel Agencies

*† **1** Which of the following services is normally provided for travellers by **both** travel agents and tour operators?

A Obtaining travellers' cheques ☐
B Obtaining passports ☐
C Obtaining travel insurance ☐
D Obtaining a visa ☐

*† **2** Which of the following usually generates the highest rate of commission for travel agents?

A Airline tickets ☐
B Hotel reservations ☐
C Travel insurance ☐
D Travellers' cheques ☐

*† **3** Which is the commonly the largest elements of retail travel agency operating costs?

A Administration ☐
B Advertising ☐
C Payroll ☐
D Premises ☐

*† **4** Which of the following statements applies to most inclusive tours?

A The longer the distance, the greater the proportion of hotel cost. ☐
B The shorter the distance, the greater the proportion of transport cost. ☐
C The longer the distance, the higher the tour operator's profit. ☐
D The shorter the distance, the lower the agent's percentage commission. ☐

*† **5** Which of the following statements is true of airlines?

A The travel agent is the only outlet for their products. ☐
B They accommodate inclusive tours. on both scheduled and charter flights. ☐
C They never have their own tour operating companies. ☐
D They charge a commission to travel agents. ☐

6 Which of the following is the most important source of revenue of most retail travel agents in northern Europe?

A Cruises ☐
B Buses and coaches ☐
C Railways ☐
D Inclusive tours ☐

7 Which of the following is the most important source of revenue of most retail travel agents in North America?

A Airlines ☐
B Buses ☐
C Car rental ☐
D Railways ☐

8 In which country are domestic rather than foreign holidays (vacations) the main source of inclusive tour sales?

A Germany ☐
B Japan ☐
C United Kingdom ☐
D United States ☐

9 In which country do retail travel agents often assemble specially tailored packages and their own brand of inclusive tours for clients?

A Germany ☐
B Japan ☐
C United Kingdom ☐
D United States ☐

10 In which country do tour operators often own both travel agencies dealing exclusively in their own products and direct mail systems?

A Germany ☐
B Japan ☐
C United Kingdom ☐
D United States ☐

7.10 Travel Trade Abbreviations

What do the following abbreviations stand for?

*† 1 ABC

....

† 2 BSP

....

† 3 DET

....

† 4 DIT

....

† 5 FET

....

† 6 FIT

....

*† 7 GIT

....

*† 8 GSA

....

*† 9 IT

....

*† 10 ITC

....

ANSWERS

7.1 Tourism as an Industry

1 A Establishments (Firms and occupations may cut across industries)

2 C To promote uniformity and comparability of official statistics.

3 C It is synonymous with tourism supply.

4 C Tourism-related industries (do not) serve only tourists.

5 A activities
B services
C foreign
6 B Conference centre ownership and management
7 C Product perishability
8 A Hotels and catering
9 B mainly from other industries into tourism industry
10 A Lateral/horizontal
B Vertical backward
C Vertical forward

7.2 Visitor Attractions Worldwide

1 A environment
B choice
C motivation
2 C The visitor experience
3 B Distance from concentrations of population
4 A Motivator
B Motivator
C Determinant
5 A Heritage sites/historic buildings
B Ancient monuments
C Industrial archaeology/heritage
6 A Admission charges
7 B Payroll
8 A Total visitors
B Income
9 A Site (Valley of the Kings)
B Event (Passion Play)
C Site (Disneyworld)
10 A National
B International
C Regional

7.3 Visitor Attractions in Britain

1 Public sector
2 Voluntary sector
3 Regional

4 National
5 'Time cars'
6 Canal boats
7 Lake District (2,280 sq.km)
8 North Yorkshire Moors (438 sq.km)
9 St Kilda
10 Gwynedd (castles and town walls dating from the region of Edward I)

7.4 Transport Models

1 Coach
2 Motor car/taxi
3 Germany
4 Italy
5 Japan
6 France
7 Catamaran
8 Hydrofoil
9 Road
10 Air

7.5 Air Transport

1 C High fixed costs (also most other transport modes)

2 B Load tonne-kilometres and capacity tonne-kilometres

3 C One who breaks a journey at an intermediate point

4 B Charter flights have higher load factors than scheduled flights

5 B Codes denoting cities/airports

6 C Warsaw Convention (1929 with subsequent amendments)

7 C Traffic rights (Third, Fourth and Fifth freedoms)

8 A Los Angeles—Honolulu

9 C growth in air transport

10 C British European Airways (BEA) and British Overseas Airways Corporation (BOAC) (1973)

7.6 Transport Synonyms and Opposites

1 return load
2 cabin baggage/hand luggage
3 stopover
4 International Load Line
5 aft/abaft
6 bow/forward
7 scheduled airline
8 port
9 air transport
10 through passenger

7.7 Hotels and Other Tourism Accommodation

1 C High investments intensity (90% or more in fixed assets)
2 A Bed occupancy
B Room occupancy
C Average room rate
3 B Building (commonly 70-80% of total investment)
4 C Payroll (commonly 30-40% of sales)
5 A Hotel room occupancies are normally higher than bed occupancies
6 B It (doest not)determine most tourists' choice of destinations
7 C 1 Hotels
A 2 Motels
B 2 Camping sites
8 B hotel classification
9

Accommodation	1	2	3
Users	B	C	A

10 C Hospitality Franchise Systems

7.8 Accommodation Types and Tariffs

1 New Zealand (North Island; called a crib in South Island)
2 France
3 Spain
4 Portugal

5 Japan
6 European Plan (EP)
7 Continental Plan (CP)
8 Bermuda Plan (BP)
9 Modified American Plan (MAP)
10 American Plan (AP)

7.9 Tour Operations and Travel Agencies

1 C Obtaining travel insurance
2 C Travel insurance (typically 30% or more)
3 C Payroll (typically around 50% or more)
4 C The longer the distance, the higher the tour operator's profit
5 B They accommodate inclusive tours on both scheduled and charter flights
6 D Inclusive tours
7 A Airlines
8 D United States
9 D Untied States
10 A Germany

7.10 Travel Trade Abbreviations

1 Advance Booking Charter
2 Band Settlement Plan
3 domestic escorted tour
4 domestic independent tour
5 foreign escorted tour
6 foreign independent tour
7 group inclusive tour
8 General Sales Agent
9 inclusive tour
10 inclusive tour charter

8 MARKETING IN TOURISM

8.1 The Marketing Concept

Note: Figures in brackets in Questions 1, 2 and 3 indicate the number of letters in the words to be inserted.

† **1** Insert the missing words in the following definition of the marketing concept by US author Philip Kotler (1991) :

The marketing concept holds that the key to achieving organizational goals consists in determining the needs and wants of A(6)......... markets and delivering the desired B (13) .... more effectively and efficiently than C (11)....................

† **2** Insert the missing words in the following definition of tourism marketing by the Swiss author Jost Krippendorf (1971) :

Marketing in tourism is to be understood as the systematic and co-ordinated execution of business policy ... to achieve the optimal A(12)..............of the needs of B(12) .... consumer groups, and in doing so to achieve an C(1!) ....return.

† **3** How are typical suppliers' responses to the following conditions in consumer markets described?

A Demand exceeding supply in a sellers' market :

(10).........................orientation

B Supply exceeding demand in a buyers' market :

(5)..........................orientation

C Supply matching demand in a buyers' market :
(9).........................orientation

*† **4** Which of the following statements is true?
A Marketing is about consumer orientation. ☐
B Marketing is synonymous with selling. ☐
C There is no need for marketing in a sellers' market. ☐

*† **5** Which of the following definitions corresponds most closely to the usage of the term 'market' in tourism?
A A place where buyers and sellers come together to do business. ☐
B Actual or potential demand for a product. ☐
C A network of dealings between the sellers and buyers of a product. ☐

† **6** Which of the following statements is true of most tourist products?
A They are composite products. ☐
B They are mostly bought as packages. ☐
C Packaging increases tourists' choice. ☐

† **7** Which of the following statements applies to most visitor attractions as elements of tourist products?
A They are invariably free. ☐
B They are a major determinant of tourists' choice of destinations. ☐
C Each destination offers *either* site *or* event attractions. ☐

† **8** Which of the following statements applies to most amenities (facilities) as elements of tourist products?
A They are invariably provided by the private sector. ☐
B They are bought by tourists individually or as part of a package. ☐
C They usually determine tourists' choice of destinations. ☐

† **9** Which of the following statements expresses most

meaningfully the concept of accessibility as an element of tourist products for marketing purposes?

A It means the physical distance in kilometres or miles to a destination from points of origin. ☐

B It is a function of external transport to a destination. ☐

C It is interpreted in terms of the time taken and/or the cost involved to reach a destination. ☐

*† **10** Marketing in tourism takes place at two levels. This means an involvement by

A tour operators and travel agents. ☐

B public and private sectors. ☐

C destination organizations and individual operators. ☐

8.2 Marketing Tools

*† **1** The elements which make up the total marketing operation of an enterprise are called

A the business mix ☐

B the marketing mix ☐

C the promotional mix ☐

D the sales mix ☐

*† **2** Market segmentation means dividing the total market into

A groups of equal size ☐

B groups of equal value ☐

C homogeneous groups ☐

D heterogeneous groups ☐

† **3** Which of the following segmentation criteria are used in psychographics?

A Life cycle ☐

B Life style ☐

C Social class ☐

D Race and religion ☐

† **4** Which of the following pairs of tourist products is likely

to be perceived as the closest substitutes by European residents?

A Beach holidays (vacations) in Greece and in Turkey ☐
B Caribbean and Mediterranean cruises ☐
C Pilgrimages to Jerusalem and to Mecca ☐
D Skiing holidays (vacations) in Austria and in Colorado, USA ☐

† **5** An omnibus survey is

A a survey using questionnaires administered to passengers on buses ☐
B a comprehensive survey which covers exhaustively all aspects of a subject ☐
C a regular repeat survey which covers a number of topics for different clients ☐
D a survey commissioned by or on behalf of a group of clients on a cost-sharing basis ☐

† **6** Which of the following approaches to product formulation reflects the marketing concept?

A Products are shaped to match competition ☐
B Products are shaped to match markets ☐
C Markets shape themselves to products ☐
D Markets and products are shaped by the external business environment ☐

7 What aspect of product formulation is particularly highlighted in Center Parc holiday (vacation) villages?

A Accommodation ☐
B Attractions ☐
C Food ☐
D Location ☐

8 Semiotics (semiology) is concerned with

A Jewish ideas and influence ☐
B conveying signs, concepts and images ☐
C scientific measurement ☐
D study of meanings ☐

*† **9** Which of the following are principals (P) and which are intermediaries (1) in the distribution of tourist products?

A Booking agencies ....
B Car rental companies ....
C Timeshare resorts ....
D Conference organizers ....

*† **10** Which of the following statements is true of retail travel agencies as distribution channels for tourist products?

A They are the only retail outlets for tourist products. ☐
B They are more important in domestic than in international tourism. ☐
C They are remunerated by a fee charged to the customer. ☐
D Their geographical distribution tends to reflect market density. ☐

8.3 Tourism Promotion

*† **1** What distinguishes publicity from other means of securing public attention?

A It seeks to influence potential customers at the point of sale. ☐
B The promoter has no control over the message. ☐
C The potential customer is known to the promote. ☐

*† **2** What distinguishes advertising from other promotion?

A The advertiser seeks to influence the potential customer at the point of sale. ☐
B The advertiser buys space or time in the media. ☐
C The advertiser has no control over the message. ☐

† **3** What distinguishes publicity and advertising from other promotion?

A They seek to influence the potential customer at the point of sale. ☐
B They are personal forms of communication. ☐
C Their function is to attract the potential customer to the point of sale. ☐

† 4 What distinguishes sales promotion from other means of attracting the potential customer?
A It always takes place away from the point of sale. ☐
B The potential customer is never known to the promoter. ☐
C It is below-the-line promotion. ☐

*† 5 What distinguishes merchandising from other promotion?
A It is an indirect method of influencing potential customers. ☐
B It seeks to influence potential customers at the point of sale. ☐
C The promoter has no control over the message. ☐

*† 6 Brochures are of major importance in tour operators' marketing communications with customers because
A they are a legal requirement in most countries ☐
B they act as a product substitute at the point of sale ☐
C they serve both as a promotional tool for the operator and as a souvenir for the customer ☐

† 7 **Net circulation** of a newspaper or periodical refers to
A the number of distributed copies ☐
B the number of sold copies ☐
C the number of people who read a copy ☐

† 8 In marketing the term **conversion rate** denotes
A the number of replies received in response to an advertisement ☐

B the ratio of customers who buy a product to the number of responses received to an advertisement ☐
C the ratio of the number of people responding to the total number approached in a survey ☐

† **9** By whom is an advertising agency normally remunerated in the conduct of a marketing campaign in respect of above-the-line advertising?
A The client ☐
B The media ☐
C The printer ☐

† **10** Which of the following may be described as **institutional promotion**?
A Direct mailing by a cruise company to members of a professional organization ☐
B Resort hotel advertising in a monthly periodical ☐
C Tourist board publicity in a generating country ☐

8.4 Pricing Methods and Approaches

What terms describe the following methods and approaches to pricing?

*† **1** Setting prices by reference to such criteria as competitors' prices and customers' attitudes, wants and preferences, and adjusting the costs and levels of service to predetermined prices

....

*† **2** Setting prices by adding a mark-up to product cost

....

*† **3** Charging different prices to different customers for the same product for reasons not associated with differences in the cost of supply

....

*† 4 Setting prices to cover the direct (variable) costs and to make a contribution to fixed costs of a product

....

† 5 Setting temporarily very low prices with the objective of driving competitors or keeping new entrants from a market

....

*† 6 Setting prices below the commonly accepted level for the product concerned

....

† 7 Keeping selling price at a stable level, *i.e.*, preventing the price from rising and avoiding price reductions

....

† 8 Setting high initial prices in markets with price-inelastic demand

....

*† 9 Setting prices with a view to achieving a predetermined rate of return on invested capital

....

*† 10 Setting specific or minimum prices for products by suppliers and requiring the distributors to sell at those prices

....

8.5 Pricing Hotel and Transport Services

What do the following abbreviations of transport fares and hotel tariffs stand for?

† 1 AP

....

† 2 APEX

....

† **3** BP

....

† **4** CP

....

† **5** EP

....

† **6** GITX

....

† **7** IPEX

....

† **8** ITX

....

† **9** MAP

....

† **10** PEX

....

8.6 Marketing Applications

† **1/2** Which of the following Caribbean tourist products can be expected to have (1) the largest market and which (2) the smallest market in Europe?

A Beach holidays (vacations) ....
B Cruising holidays (vacations) ....
C Diving holidays (vacations) ....
D Sailing holidays ....

*† **3/4** Which of the following segments is normally (3) most susceptible and which is (4) least susceptible to tourism promotion?

A Study visits ....
B Visits to friends and relatives ....
C Business visits other than

conferences ....

D Holiday (vacation) visits ....

† **5/6** Which of the following are usually perceived as (5) convenience products (CP) and which as (6) shopping products (SP) by Europeans on holiday (vacation)?

A Bank services ....

B Car rental ....

C Hotel accommodation ....

D Take-away food ....

*† **7/8** Which of the following destinations may be expected to have (7) the strongest image and which (8) the weakest image?

A Australian Barrier Reef islands among European residents ....

B Mediterranean countries among United States residents ....

C Wales among Japanese residents

....

D Scotland among Canadian residents

....

*†**9/10** Which of the following media is likely to reach (9) the largest market and which (10) the smallest market in the United States?

A A newsletter for school teachers..............................

B A national women's magazine ....

C A periodical for birdwatchers ....

D A student newspaper ....

8.7 Promotional Illustrations

What aspect of marketing is illustrated by each of the following?

*† **1** Charging lower prices in theatres to students and the retired

....

† **2** Display of travel posters in railway stations

....

† **3** Dividing an hotel market into banqueting, conferences and exhibitions

....

*† **4** Editorial mention of a resort in a periodical

....

*† **5** Grouping chain hotels with unique names and images

....

† **6** 'Happy hour' periods in bars

....

*† **7** Postal distribution of tour operator's brochure

....

† **8** 'Small ads' paid for on a line-by-line basis

....

† **9** 'Spouse-free' travel offer by an airline

....

*† **10** Tent cards on restaurant tables

....

8.8 Creative Marketing Campaigns and Messages

Name the organization identified with each of the following campaigns and messages :

1 'Have it you own way'

....

2 'I love New York'

....

3 'Only one hotel chain guarantees your room will be right'

....

4 'That'll do nicely'

....

5 'The World Next Door'

....

6 'The world's favourite airline'

....

7 'Yes, we're different'

....

8 'We speak your language'

....

9 'We try harder'

....

10 'You're the boss'

....

8.9 Marketing Synonyms and Opposites

Give a synonym for each of the following terms :

† **1** database marketing

....

*† **2** face-to-face selling

....

† **3** niche marketing

....

*† **4** point-of-sale promotion

....

† **5** telephone marketing

....

What is an opposite of each of the following terms?

*† **6** brand switching

....

*† **7** buyers' market

....

*† **8** field research

....

*† **9** market economy

....

*† **10** tactical marketing

....

8.10 Marketing Abbreviations and Acronyms

What do the following abbreviations and acronyms stand for?

† **1** AIDA

....

*† **2** CRS

....

† **3** CSQ

....

† **4** DRM

....

† **5** GDS

....

*† **6** POS

....

*† **7** PR

....

*† **8** RPM

....

*† **9** SWOT

....

† **10** USP

....

ANSWERS

8.1 The Marketing Concept

1 A target
B satisfactions
C competitors
} Kotler, P. (1991) *Marketing Management*: *Analysis, Planning and Control,* 7th edn, Englewood Cliffs NJ: Prentice Hall

2 A satisfaction
B identifiable
C appropriate
} Krippendorf, J. (1971) *Marketing et Tourisme,* Berne: Lang

3 A production
B sales
C marketing

4 A Marketing is about consumer orientation

5 B Actual or potential demand for a product

6 A They are composite products

7 B They are a major determinant of tourists' choice of destinations

8 B They are bought by tourists individually or as part of a package

9 C It is interpreted in terms of the time taken and/or the cost involved to reach a destination

10 C destination organizations and individual operators

8.2 Marketing Tools

1 B the marketing mix

2 C homogeneous groups

3 B Life style

4 A Beach holidays (vacations) in Greece and in Turkey

5 C a regular repeat survey which covers a number of topics for different clients
6 B Products are shaped to match markets
7 B Attractions (climate controlled)
8 B conveying signs, concepts and images
9 A Intermediaries
B Principles
C Principles
D Intermediaries
10 D Their geographical distribution tends to reflect market density

8.3 Tourism Promotion

1 B The promoter has no control over the message
2 B The advertiser buys space or time in the media
3 C Their function is to attract the potential costomer to the point of sale
4 C It is below-the-line promotion
5 B It seeks to influence potential customers at the point of sale
6 B they act as a product substitute at the point of sale
7 B the number of sold copies
8 B the ratio of customers who buy a product to the number of responses received to an advertisement
9 B The media
10 C Tourist board publicity in a generating country

8.4 Pricing Method and Approaches

1 Backward pricing
2 Cost-plus pricing
3 Differential pricing/price discrimination
4 Marginal cost pricing
5 Predatory pricing
6 Price cutting
7 Price pegging
8 Price skimming
9 Rate-of-return pricing
10 Resale price maintenance

8.5 Pricing Hotel and Transport Services

1 American Plan
2 Advance Purchase Excursion Fare
3 Bermuda Plan
4 Continental Plan
5 European Plan
6 Group Inclusive Tour Fare
7 Instant Purchase Excursion Fare
8 Inclusive Tour Fare
9 Modified American Plan
10 Public Excursion Fare

8.6 Marketing Applications

1 A Largest market : beach holidays (vacations)
2 C Smallest market : diving holidays (vacations)
3 D Most susceptible : holiday (vacation) visits
4 C Least susceptible : business visits
5 A/D Convenience products (CP)
6 B/C Shopping products (SP)
7 D Strongest image : Scotland among Canadian residents
8 C Weakest image : Wales among Japanese residents
9 B Largest market : a national women's magazine
10 C Smallest market : a periodical for birdwatchers

8.7 Promotional Illustrations

1 Differential pricing
2 Transport advertising
3 Product segmentation
4 Publicity
5 Branding
6 Differential pricing
7 Direct mail
8 Classified advertising
9 Sales promotion
10 Merchandising

8.8 Creative Marketing Campaigns and Messages

1 Burger King

2 New York State
3 Holiday Inn International
4 American Express
5 Tourism Canada in the USA
6 British Airways
7 British Virgin Islands Tourist Board
8 British Tourist Authority in the USA
9 AVIS
10 United Airlines

8.9 Marketing Synonyms and Opposites

1 direct response marketing
2 personal selling
3 target marketing
4 merchandising
5 telemarketing
6 brand loyalty
7 sellers' market
8 desk research
9 planned economy
10 strategic marketing

8.10 Marketing Abbreviations and acronyms

1 Attention, Interest, Desire, Action
2 computer reservation system/central reservation system
3 customer satisfaction questionnaire
4 direct response marketing
5 global distribution system
6 point of sale
7 public relations
8 resale price maintenance
9 Strengths, Weaknesses, Opportunities, Threats
10 unique selling proposition

9 PLANNING AND DEVELOPMENT IN TOURISM

9.1 Concepts in Tourism

† **1** What is considered to be the optimum approach to national tourism planning and development?

A Formulation of a national development plan with tourism as one of the sectors ☐

B Formulation of a tourism development plan ☐

C Formulation of a tourism marketing plan ☐

† **2** What is the most common sequence of tourism development in developing countries?

A Domestic tourism followed by inbound tourism ☐

B Inbound tourism followed by domestic tourism ☐

C Concurrent development of domestic and inbound tourism ☐

† **3** What is the appropriate starting point in assembling information for tourism planning and development?

A To identify available in-house information ☐

B To establish the exact purpose for which it is required ☐

C To design a survey to collect the information ☐

*† **4** The term 'community tourism' refers to

A tourism within the European Community ☐

B an approach to tourism in which local residents participate in its planning and development ☐

C group visits between 'twinned' town and cities in different countries ☐

*† 5 In tourism context the term 'carrying capacity' refers to
A capacity of a site or area ☐
B passenger capacity of a bus or coach ☐
C ship tonnage ☐

*† 6 Which of the following concurrent activities on inland waters are compatible?
A Angling and power boating ☐
B Sailing and water skiing ☐
C Swimming and scuba diving ☐

† 7 How is a land use development strategy which aims to locate particular activities, facilities and services together in an area described?
A Concentration development strategy ☐
B Cluster development strategy ☐
C Enclave development strategy ☐

*† 8 The term 'sustainable tourism' refers to
A level of tourism arrivals which can be sustained over a period of time ☐
B tourism development which commands the support of the local population ☐
C tourism activities which are in harmony with the environment in the long term ☐

*† 9 Which of the following may be classified as infrastructure and which as tourism superstructure in a resort?

A Water supply

....

B Roads

....

C Casinos

....

† **10** For which of the following is the term 'green tourism' a synonym?
A Agricultural tourism ☐
B Alternative tourism ☐
C Rural tourism ☐

9.2 Resources

† **1** It has been suggested that countries and regions should specialize in economic activities in which they have a comparative advantage. This means that they should specialize in tourism if their resources are
A better suited for tourism than other countries'/ regions' resources ☐
B better suited for tourism than for other economic activities ☐
C not suitable for any other economic activity ☐

† **2** Which of the following does **not** apply to renewable natural resources?
A They are inexhaustible. ☐
B They are capable of replenishment. ☐
C They are not vulnerable. ☐

*† **3** When referring to both natural and man-made resources, the terms conservation, preservation and restoration are often used indiscriminately. Which of the following describes the essence of conservation?
A Maintaining something in its present form ☐
B Returning something to its previous condition ☐
C Protecting something from decay and destruction ☐

† **4** A Study of new resort developments suggests that some resources receive more attention in planning stages than others. Which of the following tends to be most neglected?
A Energy resources ☐
B Manpower ☐
C Man-made attractions ☐

† 5 Which of the following activities makes least exclusive demand on land in most countries?
A Housing ☐
B Industry ☐
C Tourism ☐

*† 6 Which of the following tourism resources is of equal importance for both holiday (vacation) and for business tourism?
A Attractive scenery ☐
B Developed infrastructure ☐
C Pleasant climate ☐

*† 7 Which of the following uses of coastal resorts can be classified as tourism?
A As dormitory towns for close urban areas ☐
B As second homes ☐
C As places of retirement ☐

*† 8 Which of the following is the dominant influence on climate?
A Distribution of land and sea areas
B Latitude
C Relief

*† 9 Which of the following tourism resources is commonly provided by the public sector in developed countries?
A Accommodation ☐
B Reservation systems ☐
C Tourist information services ☐

*† 10 Which of the following is the most common multiple use of land resources?
A Agriculture and tourism ☐
B Housing and tourism ☐
C Industry and tourism ☐

9.3 Techniques, Systems and Processes

What techniques, systems or processes are used for the following purposes?

*† **1** To assess the market and financial prospects for a new project :

....

*† **2** To evaluate the anticipated costs and revenues of a project :

....

*† **3** To evaluate the benefit and the costs of a project to society :

....

† **4** To plan and monitor complex projects and activities :

....

† **5** To schedule component tasks in project planning :

....

† **6** To assess the impact of a company's activities on the environment :

....

*† **7** To assess in advance the likely environmental effects of a development project :

....

*† **8** To reduce the use of electricity, fuel and other energy resources for cost or environmental reasons :

....

*† **9** To reduce the use of water resources for cost or environmental reasons :

....

*† **10** To reduce waste for cost or environmental reasons :

....

9.4 Ownership and Management

† 1 What is a joint business venture?

A One party selling a product designed, supplied and controlled by and with the support of another party ☐

B Involvement of two or more parties in ownership, management, and operation of a business with a participation in financial outcome ☐

C Provision of organizational and operational expertise to manage a business by an operator for an agreed remuneration ☐

† 2 What is the essence of a concession?

A Control or ownership of rights to land or buildings over a certain period ☐

B Right to use land or premises on certain conditions ☐

C Provision of organizational and operational expertise to manage a business by an operator for an agreed remuneration ☐

† 3 What term describes the arrangement under which an operator takes temporary possession of a property for a specified period of time for rent payment?

A Concession ☐

B Lease ☐

C Management contract ☐

† 4 What is a management contract?

A One party selling a product designed, supplied and controlled by and with the support of another party ☐

B Involvement of two or more parties in ownership, management, and operation of a business with a participation in financial outcome ☐

C Provision of organizational and operational expertise to manage a business by an operator for an agreed remuneration ☐

† 5 What term describes the contractual relationship between two parties for the distribution of goods and services, in which one party sells a product designed, supplied and controlled and with the support of the other party?

A Franchise ☐
B Joint venture ☐
C Management contract ☐

*† 6 Which of the following groups is most interested in the balance sheet of a business?

A Management ☐
B Owners and lenders ☐
C Tax authorities ☐

*† 7 A single physical location at which one more business activities are conducted is described as

A an establishment ☐
B a firm ☐
C a partnership ☐

† 8 When a company is acquired by its staff who become shareholders, this is known as

A employee buy-out ☐
B leveraged buy-out ☐
C management buy-out ☐

† 9 What is described as dual nature of investment in hotels, means

A investment financed by equity capital and by loans ☐
B investment in land and buildings and in interior assets ☐
C investment by two different parties ☐

*† 10 What term describes a building in which the interior space of accommodation units is owned individually and the land and building in common by the owners of the individual units?

A Timeshare ☐
B Condominium ☐
C Cooperative ☐

9.5 Reshaping Existing Locations

Note : Figure in questions denote the number of letters in each area/city name.

Which resort has been 'regenerated' by, *inter alia,*

1 adding a conference centre, a marina and other facilities and attractions (in England?) : 8

....

2 changing image and product identity from a winter to a summer resort (in North Atlantic?) : 7

....

3 launching a series of festivals and other events (in England?) : 11

....

4 legalizing gambling in (in USA?) : 8, 4

....

5 transformation into a conference and day visit centre (in the Netherlands?) : 12

....

Which city has enhanced its appeal to visitors by, *inter alia,*

6 becoming a European City of Culture and an exhibition venue (in Scotland?) : 7

....

7 focusing on industrial heritage (in England?) : 8

....

8 staging several mega-events (in Canada?) : 8

....

9 rehabilitating its waterfront and other civic improvements (in Spain?) : 9

....

10 major waterfront development (in north-east USA?) : 9

....

9.6 Planning and Development Applications

1 Which of the following visitor attractions in North America is 'user-oriented'?
A Colonial Williamsburg, Virginia ☐
B Faneuil Hall, Boston, Massachusetts ☐
C Disneyworld, Florida ☐
D Niagara Falls, New York/ Ontario ☐

2 Which of the following visitor attractions in Europe is 'resource-based'?
A Fish Market, Bergen, Norway ☐
B Lake District National Park, Cumbria, England ☐
C Starnberg Lake, Bavaria, Germany ☐
D Studio Rampa Theatre, Prague, Czech Republic ☐

3 Which of the following resort areas developed largely spontaneously without much planning?
A Cancun Resort, Mexico ☐
B Nusa Dua Resort, Bali, Indonesia ☐
C South Antalya, Turkey ☐
D Venice, Itlay ☐

4 Which of the following resort areas was planned ab initio?
A Costa Brava, Spain ☐
B Cote d'Azur ☐
C Lanzarotte, Canary Islands ☐
D Pomum Lake Resort, Republic of Korea ☐

*† 5 The main reason for the decline of seaside resorts in northern Europe for domestic holidays (vacations) has been

A air and sea pollution ☐
B lack of investment ☐
C growth in holidays (vacations) in the Mediterranean ☐
D lack of promotion ☐

† 6 What effect have the growth of the inclusive tour had on the geographical distribution of holidays?

A It has brought about a wider dispersal. ☐
B It has concentrated tourists into specific locations. ☐
C It has had no particular effect. ☐

*† 7 The population drift from the land to towns in developed countries has been
A of relatively recent origin ☐
B mainly caused by tourism development ☐
C often arrested or slowed down by tourism development ☐

*† 8 Which of the following statements is **false**?
A Tourism competes with housing in some places. ☐
B Tourism provides new uses for old buildings. ☐
C Tourism destroys industrial heritage. ☐

† 9 Which of the following conservation designation schemes applies worldwide?
A Environmentally Sensitive Areas ☐
B Ramsar Sites ☐
C Special Protection Areas ☐

10 Which decade was described as the United Nations Development Decade?
A 1950s ☐
B 1960s ☐
C 1970s ☐

9.7 Planning and Development Terms

Give the appropriate term to describe each of the following :

† **1** Sale of land and building by a company to an investor

and leasing the same property back for an agreed term

....

† **2** A construction contract that leaves the contractor see to all details and hand over ran operational unit

....

*† **3** Designating area for different forms of activity

....

*† **4** A formal offer in writing to execute work or supply goods or services at an agreed price

....

*† **5** Industries supplying essential basic public services

....

*† **6** A linear building development along a road, coastline or valley

....

*† **7** Measures of government assistance to encourage firms to invest

....

† **8** Preparing proposals for, and regulating the use of land in a given area

....

† **9** Areas designated by appropriate authorities because of their archeological, cultural or environmental significance

....

† **10** The cost of an economic activity to society

....

9.8 Planning and Development Synonyms and Opposites

Give synonyms for the following terms :

† **1** alternative technology

....

*† **2** country planning

....

† **3** critical path analysis

....

† **4** timesharing

....

*† **5** urban planning

....

Give the opposites of the following terms :

† **6** enclave

....

*† **7** infrastructure

....

† **8** private cost

....

*† **9** private sector

....

*† **10** urban planning

....

9.9 Planning and Development in the UK

1 Which is the wider concept—Great Britain or United Kingdom?

....

2 The first legislation to regulate physical development in the UK was

....

3 Regulations made by public bodies such as local authorities or railway companies are called

....

4 Local authorities which combine the functions of county, borough and district councils are called

....

5 Plans which combine broad policies and detailed guidelines for some local government area are called

....

6 Areas of countryside surrounding large built-up areas in which building development is strictly controlled are called

....

7 Areas designated by central government in which businesses benefit from, *inter alia*, simplified planning procedures, are called

....

8 Statutory bodies set up by central government in order to reverse large-scale urban decline are called

....

9 Initiatives of the English Tourist Board in the 1980s to develop tourism in 'areas of potential and need', were called

....

10 The first major post World War II purpose-built recreation and tourism centre in Britain was opened at

....

9.10 Conservation Areas and Schemes in the UK **UK**

In which parts of the United Kingdom are to be found the following designated conservation areas and conservation schemes?
(✓in the appropriate column)

	England	*Scottland*	*Wales*	*N. Ireland*
1 Areas of Outstanding Natural Beauty				
2 Conservation Areas				
3 Heritage Coasts				
4 Listed Buildings				
5 National Science Areas				
6 National Nature Reserves				
7 National Parks				
8 Scheduled Ancient Monuments				
9 Sites of Special Scientific Interest				
10 Special Protected Areas				

ANSWERS

9.1 Concepts in Tourism

1 A National development plan with tourism as one of the sectors
2 B Inbound tourism followed by domestic tourism
3 B To establish the exact purpose for which it is required
4 B an approach to tourism in which local residents participate in its planning and development
5 A capacity of a site or area
6 C Swimming and scuba diving

7 B Cluster development strategy
8 C tourism activities which are in harmony with the environment in the long term
9 A Infrastructure
B Infrastructure
C Superstructure
10 B Alternative tourism

9.2 Resources

1 B better suited for tourism than for other economic activities
2 C They are (not) vulnerable
3 C Protecting something from decay and destruction
4 B Manpower
5 C Tourism
6 B Developed infrastructure
7 B As second homes (A and C denote permanent residence)
8 B Latitude
9 C Tourist information services
10 A Agriculture and tourism

9.3 Techniques, Systems and Processes

1 feasibility study
2 investment appraisal
3 Cost Benefit Analysis (CBA)
4 Programme Evaluation and Review Technique (PERT)
5 Critical Path Analysis (CAP)/network analysis
6 environmental audit
7 environmental impact assessment
8 energy management
9 water management
10 waste management

9.4 Ownership and Management

1 B Involvement of two or more parties in ownership, management and operation of a business with a participation in the financial outcome

2 B Right to use land or premises on certain conditions
3 B Lease
4 C Provision of organizational and operational expertise to manage a business by an operator for an agreed remuneration
5 A Franchise
6 B Owners and lenders (*inter alia*, in the use the business makes of its assets and in the relationship between owners' capital and loans)
7 A an establishment
8 A employee buy-out
9 B investment in land buildings and in interior assets
10 B Condominium

9.5 Reshaping Existing Locations

1 Brighton
2 Bermuda
3 Bournemouth
4 Atlantic City
5 Scheveningen
6 Glasgow
7 Bradford
8 Montreal
9 Barcelona
10 Baltimore

9.6 Planning and Development Applications

1 B Faneuil Hall, Boston, Massachusetts
2 B Lake District National Park, Cumbria, England
3 D Venice, Itlay
4 D Pomun Lake Resort, Republic of Korea
5 C growth of holidays (vacations) in the Mediterranean
6 B It has concentrated tourists into specific locations
7 C often arrested or slowed down by tourism development
8 C Tourism destroys industrial heritage
9 B Ramsar Sites
10 B 1960s

9.7 Planning and Development Terms

1. Sale and lease-back
2. Turnkey contract
3. Zoning
4. Tender
5. Public utilities
6. Ribbon development
7. Investment incentives
8. Land use planning/physical planning
9. Conservation areas/protected areas
10. Social cost

9.8 Planning and Development Synonyms and Opposites

1. appropriate technology/intermediate technology
2. rural planning
3. network analysis
4. interval ownership/multi-ownership
5. town planning
6. exclave
7. superstructure
8. social cost
9. public sector
10. rural planning

9.9 Planning and Development in the UK

1. United Kingdom (= Great Britain + Northern Ireland)
2. Town and Country Planning Act 1947
3. bylaws by-lows/byelaws
4. unitary authorities
5. unitary development plans
6. Green Belts
7. Enterprise Zones
8. Urban Development Corporations
9. Tourism Development Action Plans (TDAPs)
10. Aviemore, Scotland (in 1966)

9.10 Conservation Areas and Schemes in the UK

	England	*Scotland*	*Wales*	*N. Ireland*
1 Areas of Outstanding Natural Beauty	✓		✓	✓
2 Conservation Areas	✓	✓	✓	
3 Heritage Coasts	✓		✓	
4 Listed Buildings	✓		✓	
5 National Science Areas		✓		
6 National Nature Reserves	✓	✓	✓	✓
7 National Parks	✓		✓	
8 Scheduled Ancient Monuments	✓	✓	✓	✓
9 Sites of Special Scientific Interest	✓	✓	✓	✓
10 Special Protected Areas	✓			

10 ORGANIZATION AND FINANCE IN TOURISM

10.1 Types of Organizations in Tourism

what are the designations of the following organizations?

*† 1 Individual membership organization providing roadside and other services to motorists

....

† 2 Voluntary non-profit making association of businesses in a town or district to protect and promote their interest

....

† 3 Society providing for the survey and classification of ships

....

† 4 Voluntary group of independent firms in a particular trade or industry jointed together for marketing or other common purposes

....

† 5 Organization with institutional rather than individual membership, such as an international organization of national associations

....

† 6 Association of employees in a particular occupation to promote their common interests

....

*† 7 Association of individuals in a particular occupation, which seeks to provide status for its members, and which controls admission, usually by examination

....

*† 8 National, regional or local organization variously concerned with the development, promotion and coordination of tourism in its area

....

10.2 Governments and Tourism Organizations

† 1 Which of the following are normally central government concerns?

A Car parking ☐
B Diversification of local economics ☐
C Economic growth ☐
D Employment ☐

† 2 Which of the following are normally local government concerns?

A Balance of payments ☐
B Employment ☐
C Quality of environment ☐
D Regional balance ☐

*† 3 What is the main distinguishing feature of sectoral organizations?

A They are concerned with particular occupations. ☐
B They are concerned with particular industries. ☐
C They are concerned with tourism. ☐
D They are not concerned with tourism. ☐

† 4 Which is the oldest level of tourism organization?

A Local ☐
B Regional ☐
C National ☐
D International ☐

† **5** Which country first established a National Tourism Administration?
A France ☐
B Italy ☐
C New Zealand ☐
D Switzerland ☐

*† **6** Which of the following is the most common function of tourism destination organizations?
A Industry regulation ☐
B Manpower development ☐
C Marketing/promotion ☐
D Planning and development ☐

† **7** What is the main single reason for the involvement of tourism organizations in marketing?
A Market fragmentation ☐
B Need to promote destinations ☐
C Small scale of many operators ☐
D Spatial separation between destinations and markets ☐

† **8** Where have governments and public sector agencies most intervened directly in the development of the tourist product?
A In the First World ☐
B In the Second World ☐
C In the Third World ☐
D In the Fourth World ☐

*† **9** Which of the following policy objectives of governments and tourism organizations are least likely to conflict?
A Maximizing foreign currency earnings and regional dispersal of tourism. ☐
B Maximizing visitor numbers and conservation. ☐
C Maximizing visitor numbers and attraction of high-spending tourists. ☐
D Maximizing visitor revenue and resident employment. ☐

† **10** The major reason why the International Union of Official Travel Organizations (IUOTO), a non-governmental body, was in 1975 transformed into the World Tourism Organization (WTO), an inter-governmental body, was to
A increase membership ☐
B provide employment for government officials ☐
C draw on financial contributions of governments ☐
D influence the policies of governments in relation to tourism ☐

10.3 Organization of Tourism in the UK

1 From which year dates the beginning of central government financial support for tourism in the UK?
A 1919 ☐
B 1929 ☐
C 1939 ☐
D 1949 ☐

2 Which part of the United Kingdom had no national tourism organization before 1969?
A England ☐
B Scotland ☐
C Wales ☐
D Northern Ireland ☐

3 Which of the following UK government departments is the 'sponsor ministry' for tourism
A Education and Employment ☐
B Environment ☐
C National Heritage ☐
D Trade and Industry ☐

4 Which of the following statements describes the statutory relationship between the British Tourist Authority (BTA) and the national tourist boards for England, Scotland and Wales?
A The national boards are subordinate to BTA. ☐
B BTA is controlled by the national boards. ☐

C BTA controls the English Tourist Board but not the Scottish or the Wales Tourist Boards. ☐
D They are co-equal bodies. ☐

5 Which statutory tourist board was not created under the Development to Tourism Act 1969?
A English Tourist Board (ETB) ☐
B Scottish Tourist Board (STB) ☐
C Wales Tourist Board (WTB) ☐
D Northern Ireland Tourist Board (NITB) ☐

6 Which part of the Development of Tourism Act 1969 has not been brought into operation (by 1996)?
A Part I setting up four statutory tourist boards with defined functions and powers ☐
B Part II providing for financial assistance for hotel development ☐
C Part III providing powers for statutory registration of tourist accommodation (Section 17) ☐
D Part III providing for statutory notification of prices of accommodation (Section 18) ☐

7 Which national tourist board receives the largest amount of government grant-in-aid?
A English Tourist Board (ETB) ☐
B Scottish Tourist Board (STB) ☐
C Wales Tourist Board (WTB) ☐
D Northern Ireland Tourist Board (NITB) ☐

8 In which part of the United Kingdom has the tourism organization below national level changed from 9 regions in 1969 to 32 areas in 1983 and to 14 areas in 1995?
A England ☐
B Scotland ☐
C Wales ☐
D Northern Ireland ☐

9 In which part of the United Kingdom has the regional tourism framework changed from Regional Tourism Councils to Regional Tourism Companies?
   A England ☐
   B Scotland ☐
   C Wales ☐
   D Northern Ireland ☐

10 Which of the following sources provides the largest proportion of the income of Regional Tourist Boards in England?
   A Commercial membership ☐
   B English Tourist Board (ETB) ☐
   C Local Authorities (LAs) ☐
   D Other commercial income ☐

10.4 Tourism Organization in the UK and the Irish Republic

UK/ROI

With which parts of the United Kingdom are associated

1 Area Tourist Boards?

....

2 Regional Tourism Companies?

....

3 Regional Tourist Associations?

....

4 Regional Tourist Boards?

....

5 Tourism Development Action Plans?

....

The questions which follow refer to the Republic of Ireland.

6 Which government department is responsible for tourism?

....

7 What is the name of the national tourism organization?

....

8 How many regional tourism organizations report to the national tourism organization?

....

9 What state agency is responsible for recruitment, education and training in tourism?

....

10 What does ITIC stand for?

....

10.5 International Organizations

Which of the following are inter-governmental organizations (IGO) and which are non-governmental organizations (NGO)?

† 1 European Travel Commission (ETC)

....

*† 2 International Air Transport Association (IATA)

....

*† 3 International Civil Aviation Organization (ICAO)

....

† 4 Pacific Asia Travel Association (PATA)

....

*† 5 World Tourism Organization (WTO)

....

Which of the following statements apply to inter-governmental organizations (IGO) and which apply to non-governmental organizations (NGO)?

*† **6** Their membership consist of individuals and/or corporate bodies

....

*† **7** They are created by treaties between states.

....

† **8** They are subject to the law of the country where their headquarters are situated.

....

† **9** They are subject to international law.

....

† **10** They are sometimes able to take décisions which are binding on their members.

....

10.6 Finance in Tourism

*† 1 Finance in tourism is influenced by the political and economic system of the country. How is an economy described in which

A market forces determine what is produced?

....

B the state determines what is produced?

....

C economic activities are undertaken both by private and by public enterprise?

....

*† 2 Who normally provides infrastructure for tourism development in most countries?

A Private sector ☐
B Public sector ☐
C Voluntary sector ☐

† **3** Infrastructure investment costs of new resort developments are sometimes recovered through
- A levies on tour operators ☐
- B increased value of sites leased or sold to investors ☐
- C user fees levied on tourists ☐

† **4** Which of the following organizations tend to be most capital-intensive?
- A National Tourism Administrations ☐
- B Tourist Information Centres ☐
- C Visitor attractions ☐

† **5** What is the main direct effect of government financial incentives for tourism development, such as grants and loans?
- A Reduction of capital outlay ☐
- B Reduction of operating costs ☐
- C Winning investors' confidence ☐

† **6** What is the main direct effect of government fiscal incentives for tourism development, such as 'tax holidays'?
- A Reduction of capital outlay ☐
- B Reduction of operating costs ☐
- C Winning investors' confidence ☐

† **7** Which of the following sources accounts for most foreign investment in tourism in developed countries?
- A Foreign tour operators ☐
- B International aid agencies ☐
- C Private developers and investors ☐

*† **8** Which of the following functions accounts for the largest proportion of the expenditure of most tourism destination organizations?
- A Industry regulation ☐
- B Marketing/promotion ☐
- C Research ☐

*† 9 Who provides the largest proportion of the income of the National Tourism Administration in most countries?
- A Central government ☐
- B Tourism industry ☐
- C Tourists ☐

*† 10 What is the most common reason for governments to levy taxes on tourists?
- A Allocating the social costs of tourism to users ☐
- B Making tourism more acceptable to residents ☐
- C Raising revenue ☐

10.7 International Sources of Finance

Below are abbreviations of ten multilateral sources of finance for tourism development. Give in full the name of each organization.

1 ADB

....

2 AFESD

....

3 CABEI

....

4 CDB

....

† 5 EBRD

....

† 6 EDF

....

† 7 EIB

....

† **8** IBRD

....

9 IDB

....

† **10** IFC

....

10.8 Abbreviations of UK Organizations **UK**

What do the following abbreviations stand for?

1 ABTA

....

2 BHA

....

3 CAA

....

4 HCIMA

....

5 ILAM

....

6 NITB

....

7 PSA

....

8 RMT

....

9 WDA

....

10 YHA

....

10.9 Abbreviations of US Organizations **US**

What do the following abbreviations stand for?

1 AAA

....

2 ABA

....

3 AH&MA

....

4 ASTA

....

5 FAA

....

6 NRA

....

7 NTA

....

8 TIA

....

9 TTRA

....

10 USTOA

....

10.10 UK versus US Financial Terms **UK/US**

Give the American equivalents of the following English financial terms :

1 bank note

....

2 stock

....

3 stock turnover

....

4 debtors

....

5 creditors

....

6 shares

....

7 ordinary shares

....

8 preference shares

....

9 wages and salaries

....

10 capital gearing

....

ANSWERS

10.1 Types of Organizations

1 motoring organization (also automobile association/ club)
2 chamber of commerce
3 classification society
4 consortium/cooperative
5 federation

6 personnel association
7 professional body
8 tourist board

10.2 Governments and Tourism Organizations

1 C Economic growth
D Employment
2 B Employment
C Quality of environment
3 B They are concerned with particular industries (*i.e.* sectors)
4 A Local (based on resorts)
5 C New Zealand (1901, France 1910, France 1910, Switzerland 1917, Italy 1919)
6 C Marketing/Promotion
7 B Need to promote destinations
8 B In the Second World
9 D Maximizing visitor revenue and resident employment
10 D influence the policies of governments in relation to tourism

10.3 Organization of Tourism in the UK

1 B 1929 (grant of £5,000 by the Board of Trade)
2 A England (English Tourist Board was established in 1969)
3 C National Heritage (since 1992)
4 D They are co-equal bodies
5 D Northern Ireland Tourist Board (NITB, established under Development of Tourist Traffic Act (Northern Ireland) 1948)
6 C Part III providing powers for statutory registration of tourist accommodation (Section 17)
7 B Scottish Tourist Board (STB £18.4m, WTB £14.7m, NITB £14.7m, ETN £10.0m in 1996/97)
8 B Scotland
9 C Wales (in 1990)
10 D Other commercial income (£17.7m, ETB £5.6m, LAs £2.0m, commercial membership £2.0m in 1995/96)

10.4 Tourism Organization in the UK and Irish Republic

1 Scotland

2 Wales

3 Northern Ireland

4 England

5 England

6 Department of Transport and Tourism (since 1987)

7 Board Failte/Irish Tourist Board

8 Six (eight until 1984 when the Dublin and Eastern region were merged; in 1988 the functions of the Midwest RTO were incorporated in Shannon Development)

9 Council for Education, Recruitment and Training (CERT)

10 Irish Tourist Industry Confederation

10.5 International Organizations

1 ETC = NGO
2 IATA = NGO
3 ICAO = IGO
4 PATA = NGO
5 WTO = IGO
6 Membership of individuals and corporate bodies = NGO
7 Created by treaties = IGO
8 Subject to law of country of headquarters = NGO
9 Subject to international law = IGO
10 Able to take binding decisions = NGO

10.6 Finance in Tourism

1 A Market economy
B Planned economy
C Mixed economy
2 B Public sector
3 B Increased value of sites leased or sold to investors

4 C Visitor attractions
5 A Reduction of capital outlay
6 B Reduction of operating costs
7 C Private developers and investors
8 B Marketing/promotion
9 A Central government
10 C Raising revenue

10.7 International Source of Finance

1 African/Asian Development Bank
2 Arab Fund for Economic and Social Development
3 Central American Bank for Economic Integration
4 Caribbean Development Bank
5 European Bank for Reconstruction and Development
6 European Development Fund
7 European Investment Bank
8 International Bank for Reconstruction and Development
9 Inter-American Development Bank
10 International Finance Corporation

10.8 Abbreviations of UK Organizations

1 Association of British Travel Agents
2 British Hospitality Association
3 Civil Aviation Authority
4 Hotel and Catering International Management Association
5 Institute of Leisure and Amenity Management
6 Northern Ireland Tourist Board
7 Passenger Shipping Association
8 National Union of Rail, Maritime and Transport Workers
9 Welsh Development Agency
10 Youth Hostels Association (England and Wales)

10.9 Abbreviations of US Organizations

1 American Automobile Association
2 American Bus Association

3 American Hotel & Motel Association
4 American Society of Travel Agents
5 Federal Aviation Administration
6 National Restaurant Association
7 National Tour Association
8 Travel Industry Association of America
9 Travel and Tourism Research Association
10 United States Tour Operators Association

10.10 UK versus US Financial Terms

1 bill
2 inventory
3 inventory turnover
4 accounts receivable
5 accounts payable
6 stock
7 common stock
8 preferred stock
9 payroll
10 leverage

11 MISCELLANEOUS TOPICS

11.1 Countries and Currencies

What are the currencies of the following countries?

*† 1 Austria

....

*† 2 Denmark

....

*† 3 Germany

....

*† 4 Hong Kong

....

*† 5 India

....

*† 6 Italy

....

*† 7 Netherlands

....

*† 8 Poland

....

*† 9 Portugal

....

*† 10 Spain

....

11.2 Currencies and Countries

Which countries have the following currencies?

*† 1 Drachma

....

*† 2 Florin (F1)

....

3 Koruna (Kč/Ks)

....

4 Markka (Mk)

....

5 Naira (₦)

....

*† 6 Rand (R)

....

*† 7 Rouble/Rubl/Ruble (R)

....

8 Tolar (Slt)

....

9 Won

....

*† 10 Yen

....

11.3 Employment Terms

What term describes

*† 1 employment on one's own account, with or without any employees?

....

*† **2** working in one or more jobs in addition to one's normal employment?

....

*† **3** economic activities not declared for taxation purposes?

....

† **4** not declaring one's employment for taxation purposes?

....

† **5** working from home using information technology?

....

What term describes an employment arrangement under which

† **6** a person is employed by the hour or on a day-to-day basis?

....

† **7** each employee can choose within limits his/her working hours?

....

† **8** a full-time job is performed by more than one person each working part-time?

....

*† **9** two working periods separated by a long interval?

....

*† **10** the total number of hours over which word extends in a day exceeds the number of hours worked?

....

11.4 Nautical Terms

Give the nautical terms for the following :

*† **1** rear of a ship

....

*† **2** front of a ship

....

*† **3** middle part of a ship

....

*† **4** left side of a ship

....

*† **5** right side of a ship

....

6 sheltered side of a ship (against wind)

....

7 least sheltered side of a ship (against wind)

....

8 depth of the bottom of a ship below the water surface

....

9 breadth of a ship at its widest point

....

10 at right angles to the length of a ship

....

11.5 Food and Catering Terms

What term describes the following?

*† **1** Food fulfilling requirements of Jewish law

....

† **2** Food fulfilling requirements of Muslim law

....

*† **3** Food partially or fully prepared by the manufacturer and used as labour-saving alternative to raw food

....

*† 4 Limited choice menu with a single price for any combination of items chosen or with a price determined by the choice of the main dish

....

*† 5 Menu providing a choice of items, each of which is priced separately

....

*† 6 Meal served between normal breakfast and lunch times and replacing breakfast and lunch

....

† 7 Style of restaurant table service in which food is portioned and plated in the kitchen

....

† 8 Trolley from which final preparation and service of a dish is performed in a restaurant

....

† 9 Style of restaurant table service in which portioned food is served from silver salvers placed on a gueridon

....

† 10 Place where a number of different food outlets share a common eating area

....

11.6 Airlines and Hotels, 1945-1995

At various times since the end of World War II airlines have owned hotels. The first column below lists ten such airlines and the second column the hotel companies which were or still are owned by them. Show in the space below the hotel company owned by each of the airlines.

1 Aer Lingus	**A** Ana Enterprises
2 Air France	**B** Copthorne Hotels
3 Air India	**C** Sunwing Hotels

4 All Nippon Airways
5 Japan Airlines
6 Pan American
7 SAS
8 TWA
9 United Airlines
10 VARIG

D Hilton International
E Hotel Corporation of India
F Inter-Continental Hotels
G Meridien Hotels
H Nikko Hotels International
I Tropical Hotels
J Westin Hotels

Airline	1	2	3	4	5	6	7	8	9	10
Hotel co.										

11.7 Tourism and Technology

What term describes

† **1** the first system for high speed electronic transmission of an exact copy of a document between locations?

† **2** electronic services which display transmitted information on a video screen?

† **3** an electronic communication system in which money is transferred between accounts through terminals in retail outlets and computers in banks?

† **4** a system in which cards issued by airlines enable passengers to obtain a boarding card from a machine at the airport?

† **5** computer simulation which attempts to replace the user's experience of the physical world with three-dimensional effects?

Which computer reservation system (CRS)

6 is owned jointly by Air France, Iberia and Lufthansa?

7 is owned in part by QANTAS?

8 is owned by American Airlines?

9 was formed as a joint venture between DATAS II and PARS systems in 1990?

10 merged with the Galileo network to form Galileo International in 1992?

11.8 US versus UK Language **US/UK**

Give the English equivalents of the following American terms :

1 bed and board

....

2 bypass

....

3 cutting in line

....

4 in-plant travel agency

....

5 interval ownership

....

6 one-way ticket

....

7 slip

....

8 subway

....

9 truck shop

....

10 ZIP code

....

11.9 UK Leaders in the Tourism Industry

In the UK, which

1 is the largest airline?

....

2 airport handles the most passengers?

....

3 is the longest pleasure pier?

....

4 is the largest charter airline?

....

5 is the largest cross-Channel ferry operator?

....

6 is the biggest hotel?

....

7 hotel company has the largest market share?

....

8 tour operator has the largest market share?

....

9 travel agency has the most retail outlets?

....

10 attraction has the largest number of visitors?

....

11.10 World Leaders in the Tourism Industry

Which is the world's

1 largest airline?

....

2 busiest airport?

....

3 biggest passenger ship?

....

4 biggest hotel?

....

5 airport handling most international passengers?

....

6 largest restaurant company?

....

7 largest shopping complex?

....

8 largest employer?

....

9 biggest sea ferry?

....

10 attraction with most visitors?

....

ANSWERS

11.1 Countries and Currencies

1 Schilling (s)
2 Danish Krone (Kr)
3 Deutsche Mark (DM)
4 Hong Kong Dollar (HK$)
5 Indian Rupee (Rs)
6 Italian Lira (L)
7 Netherlands Guilder (F1)
8 Zloty
9 Portuguese Escudo (Esc)
10 Spanish Peseta (Pta)

11.2 Currencies and Countries

1 Greece
2 Netherlands (Guilder)
3 Czech Republic/Slovakia
4 Finland
5 Nigeria
6 South Africa

7 Belarus/Russian Federation/Tajikistan
8 Slovenia
9 North and South Korea
10 Japan

11.3 Employment Terms

1 Self-employment
2 Moonlighting
3 Black/hidden/informal economy
4 Ghosting
5 Teleworking
6 Casual/occasional employment
7 Flexitime
8 Job sharing
9 Split shift
10 Spreadover of hours

11.4 Nautical Terms

1 (ab) aft/(a) stern
2 bow/forward/prow
3 (a) midship (s)
4 port
5 starboard
6 leeward
7 windward
8 draft/draught
9 beam
10 abeam

11.5 Food and Catering Terms

1 kosher
2 halal
3 convenience food
4 table d'hote menu
5 a la carte menus
6 brunch
7 American service/plate service
8 gueridon

9 French service
10 food court (also hawker centre in South-East Asia)

11.6 Airlines and Hotels, 1945-1995

Airline	1	2	3	4	5	6	7	8	9	10
Hotel co.	B	G	E	A	H	F	C	D	J	I

Aer Lingus	Copthorne Hotels
Air France	Meridien Hotels
Air India	Hotel Corporation of India
All Nippon Airways	Ana Enterprises
Japan Airlines	Nikko Hotels International
Pan American	Inter-Continental Hotels
SAS	Sunwing Hotels
TWA	Hilton International
United Airlines	Westin Hotels
VARIG	Tropical Hotels

11.7 Tourism and Technology

1 Facsimile transmission/fax
2 Videotex
3 Electronic funds transfer
4 Electronic ticketing
5 Virtual reality
6 Amadeus
7 Fantasia
8 Sabre
9 Worldspan
10 Apollo

11.8 US versus UK Language

1 full board/en pension
2 direct selling
3 queue jumping
4 in-house travel agency
5 timesharing
6 single ticket

7 berth
8 underground railway
9 transport café
10 post code

11.9 UK Leaders in the Tourism Industry

1 British Airways
2 London Heathrow (54.1 million terminal passengers in 1995)
3 Southend-on-Sea Essex (2.15km long; longest pier in the world)
4 Britannia Airways (owned by Thomson Corporation together with Thomson Holidays and Lunn Poly)
5 P&O (announced merger with Stena, second largest, in 1996; merger referred to Monopolies & Mergers Commission)
6 London Forum Hotel (in Cromwell Road, with accommodation for up to 1,856 guests in 910 rooms)
7 Forte (market share 20% + of hotel rooms in 1995, acquired by Granada in 1996)
8 Thomson Holidays (estimated market share 30% in 1995)
9 Lunn Poly (800 retail outlests in 1996, Going Places 700+, A.T. Mays 400+, Thos. Cook 400)
10 Blackpool Pleasure Beach (with 7.4 million visitors in 1995)

11.10 World Leaders in the Tourism Industry

1 Delta Airlines (carried 87 million passengers in 1995 on 4,800 daily flights to 48 US States and 31 countries)
2 Chicago O'Hare (handle 67.3 million passengers in 1995)
3 *Norway* (Norwegian Cruise Line flagship 315m long with a capacity of 2,022 passengers and 9000 crew)
4 MGM Grand Hotel/Casino in Las Vegas, Nevada, USA (with 5,005 rooms)
5 long Heathrow (46.8 million international passengers in 1995)

6 McDonald's International (owned and licensed 18,380 restaurants in 89 countries at the end of 1995)
7 West Edmonton Mall, Alberta, Canada (recorded 20 million shoppers in 1995)
8 Indian Railways (with 1.6 million employees in 1995)
9 *Silja Europa* between Stockholm, Sweden and Helsinki, Finland (can carry 3,000 passengers, 350 cars and 60 lorries)
10 Walt Disney World/Epcot Center, Florida, USA)

12 DESTINATIONS IN TOURISM

Introduction

Branding is perhaps the most powerful marketing weapon available to contemporary destination marketers confronted by increasing product parity, substitutability and competition. Today most destinations have superb five-star resorts, hotels and attractions, every country claims a unique culture and heritage, each place describes itself as having the friendliest people and the most customer-focused tourism industry and service, and facilities are no longer differentiators. Such is the substitutability of tourism destinations that, for example, UK tourists in search of a moderately prices sun and sand experience will accept a range of alternatives—from resorts in Cyprus, to those in Turkey, Spain or Greece. As a result, the need for destinations to create a unique identity—to differentiate themselves from their competitors—is more critical than ever. Indeed, it has become *the* basis for survival within a globally competitive marketplace where, for instance, a destination such as New Zealand competes with approximately ninety other destinations for only 30 per cent of the worldwide tourism market (Piggott, 2001 : 79). Yet, despite this aggressive marketplace, how many country advertisements do you see which portray blue seas, cloudless skies and endless golden beaches with a less than memorable tag line? Yet what does differentiate one Caribbean or Mediterranean island from its nearest neighbour? Rarely sun and sand. In this marketplace what persuades potential tourists to visit (and revisit) one place instead of another is whether they have empathy with the destination and its values. The battle for customers in tomorrow's destination marketplaces will be fought not over price but over hearts and minds—and this is where we move into the realm of branding.

In marketing terms a brand represents a unique combination of product characteristics and added values, both functional and non-functional, which have taken on a relevant meaning which is inextricably linked to that brand, awareness of which might be conscious or intuitive (Macrae, Parkinson and Sheerman, 1995). Brand advantage is secured through communication which highlights the specific benefits of a product, culminating in an overall impression of a superior brand. The image the product creates in the consumer's mind, how it is *positioned*, however, is of more importance to its ultimate success than its actual characteristics. Brand managers positions their brands so that they are perceived by the consumer to occupy a niche in the marketplace occupied by no other brand—thus, for marketers, the value of a successful brand lies in its potential to reduce substitutability. Brand managers differentiate their product by stressing attributes they claim will match their target markets' needs more closely than other brands and then they create a product image consistent with the perceived self-image of the targeted consumer segment (Schiffman and Kanuk, 2000). When consumers make brand choices about products—including destinations—they are making lifestyle statements since they are buying into not only an image but also an emotional relationship (Sheth, Mittal and Newman, 1999; Urdde, 1999). Consumers have their own 'brand wardrobes from which they make selections to communicate, reflect and reinforce associations statements and memberships; in effect, 'consumers enrobe themselves with brands, partly for what they do, but more for what they help express about their emotions, personalities and roles' (de Chernatony, 1993 : 178).

Given the nature of this brand-consumer relationship, there is increased focus among marketers on differentiation through loyalty and the emotional appeal of brands, rather than through discernible, tangible benefits (Westwood *et al.*, 1999). As Lury (1998 : 4) says 'it is our perceptions—our beliefs and our feelings about a brand that are most important'. However, mere emotion is not enough, the key is to develop a strong brand which holds some *unique* association for the consumer—while emotion has always been an important component of branding, emotion in the absence of a point of difference that can be articulated and firmly seated in the memory is arguably a recipe for consumer confusion' (Hallberg, 1995). Such is the importance of this product positioning that it have been described as the essence of marketing and, since it conveys how the product will satisfy a consumer need, different consumer meanings can be assigned to the same product via different positioning strategies, depending on the audience and stage in the brand life cycle.

The Challenges of Destination Branding

No matter where destinations are in the life cycle, they all face a number of marketing challenges. Most national tourism organizations have limited budgets and yet they have to market globally, competing not just with other destinations, but also with other global brands. Procter & Gamble, the world's biggest advertiser, may spend millions each year promoting their various brands but countries such as Spain, France and Thailand still have to vie with them for consumer mindshare in a crowded environment characterized by spiralling media costs. While one corporate giant such as Sony would spend in excess of US$300 million on its annual advertising globally, the World Tourism Organization (WTO) estimates that the world's governments are currently spending around US$350 million each year on destination advertising—accounting for around half of the promotional budgets of national tourism organizations. Table 12.1 illustrate the biggest advertising spenders at the end of the 1990s (other significant spenders included Greece, Turkey, Egypt and Canada)—not, of course, including private sector spending. It is worth pointing out here that this table only illustrate *national* advertising spend—where available. It does not, for instance, include countries which have no national tourism organization. In the USA, for sample state promotion is undertaken by a variety of convention bureaux and state travel offices—whose budgets often exceed those of some countries. The Illinois state travel office budget in 1997 topped US$35 million, that of Texas was

US$25 million and Pennsylvania almost US$20 million. Compare these figures with the national tourism budgets of Germany (US$27 million), Hungary (US$21 million) and Morocco (US$18 million) (Lurman, 1998). A recent CNN research survey (March 2000) showed that some US$538 million was spent on destination marketing alone in the USA during 1999 (Piggott, 2001 : 10).

Thus, the first challenge facing destination marketers is their extremely limited budgets by comparison with the marketers of many consumer goods and services. Combine this with evidence that tourism promotion does not *persuade* uncommitted potential vacationers (but rather acts to *confirm* the intentions of those already predisposed to visit), and destination managers and their advertising agencies have genuine problems. So how can destination marketers compete with the mega-consumer brands and penetrate the fog of advertising overload? Clearly they have to *outsmart* rather than *outspend* the competition—and that means creating innovative, attention-grabbing advertising on a budget *and maximizing* the media spend. This is a simple, self-evident truth but in destination advertising it is extremely difficult to achieve. This is not to say that destination marketers are not good at their jobs, but that effective place branding is often compromised by the *politics* of destination advertising.

Table 12.1. Top National Tourism Organizations' Advertising Spend, 1997

Country	*Advertising spend (US$ millions)*
Australia	30
Thailand	26
Cyprus	17
Spain	17
France	16
Puerto Rico	16
Brazil	15
Portugal	13

Source : WTO (figures to nearest million).

The Challenge of Politics

Successful destination branding is about achieving a balance between applying cutting-edge advertising and public relations approaches to a marketing problem and the realpolitik of managing local, regional and national politics. This is the second challenge for destination marketers and the real success stories reflect destination brands which have been able to resist the political dynamic (which is exerted at all levels of the political scene). These are brands which have strong advertising heritages, are consistent but at the same time which evolve, move with the times and appear continually contemporary and fresh. This is easy to write but difficult to achieve and that is why the same destinations are constantly cited as classic examples of cohesive, long-term branding—because they are a rare breed and they succeed against the odds. Thus, Ireland has been running the same basic proposition in its various campaigns for decades and while marketing directors and executives change the message remains constant—currently encapsulated in the *'Live a different life'* strap line.

Certainly, nowhere is the paradox of public policy and market forces more sharply defined than in destination branding. For instance, there is considerable debate among destination marketers and destination stakeholders over the use of cliches and stereotypes in marketing and advertising. Often consumers have very cliched images about countries, yet those cliches are frequently disliked in the countries themselves. One view is if the consumer connects with a cliché about a country, then its marketers should use it since it has recognition and therefore advertising value. That, however, is an agency view—not one tempered by the experience of seeing the media fallout of an advertising campaign perceived by residents as perpetuating stereotypes which are (by definition) outdated caricatures of places and peoples. The answer—which is both politically acceptable and which makes marketing sense—is to craft images which use the cliche as a hook on which to hang more detail; the narrow, cliched identity can then be reshaped and given greater complexity and richness through effective and consistent marketing.

Beyond such issues, public sector destination marketers are also hugely hampered by a variety of political pressures—they have to reconcile a range of local and regional interests and promote an identity acceptable to a range of constituencies (Buhalis, 2000). Some of the reasons why Brand Oregon, designed to be inclusive of tourism and economic development, began to fall apart in the late 1980s included : the tourism sector's resistance to direction from the top; the failure by some economic development organizations to see the connections between Oregon's lifestyle and business opportunities; and the tourism regions' reluctance to produce advertising and publications consistent with the state's branded campaign (Curtis, 2001 : 76-7). In addition to such compromising of the creative process of marketing destinations, destination brand building is also frequently undermined by the short-termism of the tourism organizations' political masters. A destination brand's lifespan is a longer-term proposition than the careers of most politicians and Julie Curtis of the Oregon Tourism Commission urges destination marketers to 'stay the course', and resist making changes too quickly since 'it takes many years to establish a brand image, establish name recognition and develop strong awareness of a destination or product' (Curtis, 2001 : 81).

Bureaucratic red tape can also confound effective advertising—the marketers of Valencia, Spain's third city, for instance, are obliged to issue new advertising contracts every year—a practice which can do little to ensure consistency of message. Frequently, political considerations within a local state can even dictate the range of photographs which are included in a campaign. Many a creative execution has had to be amended so that brochures, commercials or posters can include photographs to illustrate *all* the key areas, towns or resorts within a region or country. While this has its political advantages in that it appeases local pressure groups and local residents—and politicians are vulnerable to bad press and unrest in the trade—it will seriously compromise the impact of the branding campaign. As Bob Garfield, editor of Advertising Age and long-time advertising critic, has said of destination advertising : 'When you look at the ads ...you can see transcripts of the arguments at the tourist boards ...the membership of which all wanted their own interests served ...you can see the destruction of the advertising message as a result of the polities' (Garfield, 1998).

Even when all the internal stakeholders are satisfied with a campaign, destination branding can run into political problems as a result of external pressures. Perhaps one of the most depressing examples of this was the 'Feast for the Senses' brand created by Publicis for the Morocco Tourist Board in the mid-1990s. The campaign was an attempt to craft a homogeneous brand identity for the country in all its generating markets—each of which had previously commissioned quite separate advertising on the reasonable premise that consumers in the UK, Germany, France, Italy, etc. all sought different experiences from a holiday to Morocco. Yet this disparate approach had created a blurred and confused image of the country. Working with the Morocco Tourist Board—whose total annual tourism budget was approximately US$18 million (Lurham, 1998)—the agency therefore decided to create a new logo and produced a number of stunning visuals in a series of ten posters and in the main brochure, followed through in television commercials—all based around the strap line 'Morocco—A Feast for the Senses'. All the advertising was produced in the key markets' languages, so while consistency of brand image was achieved, the local Morocco marketing office in each of the markets was to some extent free to choose the visual it thought would best reflect the country's most marketable brand values in that particular country.

Each of Morocco's main tourism regions was featured in the campaign, and such was the positive reaction in Morocco itself when the visuals were seen that in the next phase the agency even created posters for those areas where there was little or no tourism infrastructure. Yet, while the brand-building exercise was warmly welcomed in Morocco—and actually began to change regional policy-makers' attitudes to the potential of tourism—it proved extremely difficult to sell the idea to external stakeholders. Travel agents and tour operators had to be persuaded to embrace it and a considerable effort was put into trade promotional packs, including displays, maps and a new trade magazine. Ultimately the campaign hit problems because German tour operators lobbied the Morocco Tourist Board, concerned that the brand was promoting the country as a cultural destination and not as the sun and sea product which their customers were seeking. While the visuals and the logo were retained in the following year, Publicis lost the contract and the dilution of the strong brand values of the original concept began (Vial, 1997).

The Challenge of the External Environment

While all products are affected by external change, destinations are particularly vulnerable to international politics, economics, terrorism and environmental disasters. The Gulf War, volcanic eruptions and hurricanes in the Caribbean, the Asian economic collapse, political instability in Fiji, oil spills off the Galapagos Islands and the UK foot and mouth outbreak are just some of the recent crises which have derailed destination promotional planning. One destination which has seen its promising branding activities undermined by political change is Israel. In the UK, Israeli marketing has fallen into three distinct phases since 1993. Phase One (1993-8) saw the launch of marketing activities designed to enable Israel to stand out from the crowd. Phase Two (1999-2000) saw Israel make maximum capital out of its links with the Judaeo-Christian Millennium celebrations. Phase Three (2000 onwards) has seen the country's branding activities seriously compromised by the breakdown of the peace process, and today images of the country are again associated with violence and sectarianism. In 1993 Israel was a poor performer in the UK—acknowledged as perhaps the world's most competitive travel market. Research in the UK among Israel's primary target market (upper-and middle-income groups aged twenty-five to sixty) revealed that Israel scored very poorly in terms of people's future (next twelve months) holiday consideration set—considerably below competitors such as Italy and Greece, and well below Spain. Perhaps of even greater concern were the perceptions held among consumers in its target market. Israel was variously seen as a third world country, a desert, a place only for religious fanatics and last (but by no means least) a war zone. The one piece of good news, however, was that these perceptions did not cause people to totally reject the possibility of holidaying in Israel—a potential further boosted by the 1993 peace accord.

Between 1993 and 1998 Israeli advertising in the UK sought to present the country in a very positive and memorable light and, significantly, the Israeli national tourist office was prepared to make additional funds available to stimulate visitor growth—working with a total promotional budget of around $24 million, just under half of which was allocated to advertising (Lurham, 1998). Targets were set to achieve a 30 per cent increase in tourism arrivals in two years, aiming to move from attracting 230,000 to 300,000 UK visitors. At that time, visitors to Israel fell into three categories—the Jewish community (30 per cent), Christian pilgrims (20 per cent) and the upscale market (50 per cent). The last group were felt to offer the greatest opportunities for the growth demanded by the national tourist office (NTO). Within this target market, the advertising would specifically target couples aged twenty-five to thirty-five, without children, followed by the fifty-plus empty-nesters. The advertising needed to communicate that Israel was not a cheap nor a young sun and sand destination; it also needed to overcome the target markets' misconceptions. Israel was therefore branded as a 'Quality beach holiday offering the texture and atmosphere of the Mediterranean but with a rich heritage and exotic overtones'. The keys to the detail of this positioning were the quality of its four—and five-star hotels and service, its varied beaches and seas (the Red, Dead, Mediterranean and Galilee Seas), its year-round sunshine and activities, and its Mediterranean quality in tone and sophistication (rather than geography). However, the positioning needed to be communicated via a strong, simple, memorable and unique brand hook.

The final destination advertising combined 'Hava Nagila' (an Israeli folk song well known in the UK) with the concept that people want a great holiday. Hence, the strap line : 'HAV'A Great Holiday in Israel' was used in all advertisements. The campaign used television, press and poster advertisements, all focusing on the London and South East region. The 'Hava Nagila' folk song was central to the executions in every medium, being used as the musical accompaniment and also the hook for each scene change in the television commercials, as well as providing the inspiration for the copy in the posters and the main brochure—for example, 'HAV'A trip to Jerusalem' and 'HAV'A great holiday'. In the poster advertisements 'HAV'A' (displayed in bold central type) linked two separate—although linked—images, for instance, gold beaches and golden Jerusalem; each execution invited tourists to submerge themselves in the country's culture and history as well as its scenery.

The campaign performed remarkably well and, in just one year, the growth target of 30 per cent was achieved and then maintained in subsequent years. While the total winter sun market in the UK grew by 7 per cent in 1993/4, Israel's grew by 18 per cent and Eilat (one of Israel's key resorts) by 34 per cent. Israel's spontaneous awareness levels increased dramatically on pre-and post-measures, and exceeded the post-awareness levels of all its competitors. The advertising itself became famous and distinctive in a market notorious for its uniformity and lack of brand differentiation, and prompted advertising recall grew from 38 per cent in 1993 to 50 per cent in 1994 and reached 57 per cent in 1996 despite a decreasing advertising budget (Rodwell, 1999).

In 1999-2000 the 'HAV'A' campaign was suspended while Israel capitalized on the opportunities created by the Millennium, with the intention that the new campaign would provide the ideal platform for further branding opportunities based on its positioning of Israel as a Mediterranean destination with culturally exotic overtones. In the Judaeo-Christian world, no country had a stronger link with or claim to the Millennium than Israel and central to this positioning was the need to communicate with Israel's ethnic and religious market, as well as its mainstream holiday market. The destination advertising needed to speak to all people who, for whatever reason, were thinking about the Millennium in an *emotional* way. It needed to show why Israel should be considered as a destination, its inherent magic and, of course, its relevance to the Millennium.

Central to the proposition created by Israel's advertising agency (Court Burkitt and Company of London) was 'the best Millennium experience is surely where it all began'. A series of poster advertisements were produced for the UK market which invited the tourist to Israel while juxtaposing Israel's claims with those of other less 'worthy' destinations in which to celebrate the new Millennium. One execution headlined, 'In the year 2000 do you really want to say you went to Florida?', against a shot of three camels silhouetted against a glorious sunset. In a similar vein, another poster featured a beautifully shot scene of divers in the Red Sea with the copy : 'The Millennium and it's not just 2000 years of history you'll want to dive into.' A further poster asked, 'Can you really experience the Millennium in SE10?' above a photograph of Jerusalem's skyline and Jerusalem's dome commemorating the place where the prophet Elijah is said to have ascended in to heaven. This poster had particular meaning in the UK market as it contrasted the Jerusalem temple dome with the Millennium Dome—located in SE10 (Rodwell, 1999).

The marketing success of this development of the Israel brand has, however, been dealt a serious, if not fatal blow by the recent collapse of the peace process. Images of conflict, unrest and sectarian violence are once again regularly featured on the world's news bulletins, and international tourist arrivals have declined as a result. Israeli tourism has, of course, recovered from a series of such setbacks in the past and it remains to be seen how it responds to this latest challenge. The lesson from this case study, however, is that even a well-funded, internally supported branding exercise cannot guarantee success, such is the unpredictability of the external marketing environment.

The Challenge of the Destination Product

Examples of countries being influenced by external pressures to adapt and change their marketing activities, or whose marketing is seriously compromised by events outside their marketers' control, highlight the fact that destinations are not a single product but composite products consisting of a bundle of different components including : accommodation and catering establishments; tourist attractions : arts, entertainment and cultural venues; and the natural environment (Buhalis. 2000 : Ritchie and Crouch, 2000). Destination marketers have relatively little control over these different aspects of their product and a diverse range of agencies and companies are partners in the task of crafting brand identities. These could include local and national government agencies, environmental groups and agencies chambers of commerce, trade associations and civic groups. While packaged goods normally have an obvious core—so that their advertisements can anchor themselves to product performance and attributes—with destinations the situation is much less clear (Morgan and Pritchard, 1998; 1999).

The essence of creating a successful brand is to build an emotional link between the product and the consumer, but what encapsulates the emotional brand values of a destination? Is it the atmosphere of a resort, the hotel the tourist stays in, the friendliness of the local people or some overall impression (Tapachai and Waryszak. 2000)? All of these factors can and do affect how the tourist views the vacation experience. In view of the fact that it is a composite product, can a destination ever evoke high levels of emotional commitment? Obviously, we would argue that it can as the potential to evoke an emotional attachment is even greater for tourism destinations than for fast-moving consumer goods (fmcg) or services—destinations have very strong and pervasive associations for tourists which, if skilfully orchestrated, can provide the basis for brand building (Baloglu and Brinberg, 1997). Today's tourists are not asking 'what can we do on holiday?', but 'who can we be on holiday?'—they are increasingly looking less for escape and more for discovery—and that creates the basis of an emotional connection which marketers can exploit through branding (Morgan and Pritchard, 2000 : 278. The challenge beyond that is to make the destination brand live, so that visitors truly experience the promoted brand values and feel the authencity of a unique place.

The Challenge of Creating Differentiation

While there are these added pressures in destination marketing, effective branding can still be accomplished. As Bob Garfield (1998) notes : 'Smart managers find out what is the meaning of their destination as a product to their potential consumer. They exploit that meaning in finding the value they can add to the sun and sand experience. Their advertising, when it's done well, should reflect that added value...that point of differentiation.'

Most destinations have something—a unique selling opportunity—that can be translated into a unique selling proposition. The US Virgin Islands, for example, are a sun, surf and sand destination which is physically identical to the British Virgin Islands which are 40 nautical miles away. Yet, because the US Virgin Islands' biggest market is the USA, they do have something on which to build a unique proposition. Marketers can advertise the concept that US visitors can have the exotic experience of a natural paradise—yet with the comfort and security of visiting somewhere where everyone speaks their language and uses their currency. For those Americans who want a beach holiday and are predisposed to try something partly exotic but mostly safe and familiar, the US Virgin Islands have a unique opportunity and hence marketers use the strap lines 'They're your islands' and 'The American Paradise in the Caribbean'. These differentiate the destination from the British Virgin Islands, which use the phrases 'Out of this world...not out of reach' and 'Nature's Little Secrets'. As the US Virgin Islands' brochure points out :

> As an American territory, the US Virgin Islands offers United States citizens significant advantages over other Caribbean vacation getaways. Even if you are an international traveller, you will find the American system of laws and customs under which the US Virgin Islands operates to be convenient and trouble-free ...The US Virgin Islands. They're your islands. Come see them for yourself and you'll find yourself returning.

Countries often promote their history, their culture and their beautiful scenery in their marketing, but many destinations have these attributes and it is critical to build a brand on something which uniquely connects a destination to the consumer now or has the potential to do so in the future. It must also be a proposition which the competition wants and is may be able to *copy* but which they cannot *surpass or usurp*. For example, other world cities can claim to be romantic or spiritual, but only Rome (or more strictly, the Vatican) is 'The Eternal City'—it has that epithet, it had it first and no other place can now claim it. Virginia in the USA has had phenomenal success with its 'Virginia is for Lovers' campaign but no destination can surpass Paris for its associations with romance. Whatever proposition is used it must also have the potential to last, to grow old and to evolve in a long-term branding campaign, so it is essential to get it right. However, the point of differentiation must reflect a promise which can be delivered and which matches expectations. Good destination branding is therefore original and different but its originality and difference needs to be *sustainable, believable* and *relevant* not, for instance, as in the case of Philadelphia, USA, whose promise about your vacation memories of the place living with you forever probably promises too much.

One such destination marketing campaign which transcended the commodity nature of the product and which promised a unique (yet credible) experience was the 'India Changes You' campaign of 1998. There are many exotic countries which a consumer could visit and most of them have breath-taking scenery and fascinating heritage, yet such is the emotional power of the subcontinent with its poignant history and diverse cultures that the advertising promise to the consumer that 'India changes you' is sustainable. Garfield (1998) has described this campaign premise as 'among the most powerful advertising statements I have ever encountered in any category anywhere—it's not "get away from it all", it's not "escape the rat race", it's not "discover yourself—which are all fairly familiar themes—it's better than discover yourself, it's "change yourself." It's breathtaking'. The brand proposition was only a part of the reason for this campaign's success. The other was that in this instance, the marketers of India also managed to transcend the politics of tourism advertising. Despite the fact that India is made up of a number of enormously populous regions, all competing for tourism business, the campaign promoted the whole of India as one destination and, in doing so, succeeded in preventing any dilution of the advertising message which the promotion of the individual regions would have created.

Branding Destinations : Making it Happen

As we have seen, limited budgets, the lack of overall product control and internal and external pressures pose unique challenges for destination marketers. In such circumstances, the creation of brand saliency—the development of an emotional relationship with the consumer through highly choreographed and focused communications campaigns—holds the key to destination differentiation (see, for example, Anholt, 1999; Crockett and Wood, 1999; Hall, 1999; Nickerson and Moisey, 1999; Curtis, 2001). In the 1980s there were several highly successful marketing campaigns which centred on a consistent communications proposition. New York's 'I love NY' and the 'Glasgow's miles better' campaigns are two of the best known. In these, and in many other instances, the campaigns focused on logos and slogans but they were not truly *branding* initiatives. In building a brand for a destination the identity creation should not be confined to the visual, and this is the essence of 'mood brand marketing'. It is designed to create an emotional relationship between the destination and potential visitors—as in the current 'Amazing Thailand' and '100% New Zealand' campaigns. In both, the branding activities concentrate on conveying the essence or *the spirit* of the destination, often communicated via a few key attributes and associations.

Not to be confused with any religious connotations, this is marketing based very much on an emotional or spiritual appeal (Morgan and Pritchard, 2000). If successful, such activities do not only have an impact on how the rest of the world regards a place but also on a destination's view of itself. This has very much been the case in Australia, for instance. Here, the achievements of the Sydney 2000 Olympic Games (in sporting, marketing, operations management and facility design terms), coupled with the ongoing aggressive branding of the country as a whole, has created a new view of Australia as a cosmopolitan, outward-looking country, and many of the country's politicians see Sydney 2000 as symbolizing the modernization of the Australian economy (Morse, 2001; Tibbott, 2001). It has been estimated that the exposure gained through hosting the Games accelerated Australia's marketing by ten years and that they will generate an additional A$6.1 billion in foreign exchange earnings between 1997 and 2004. Moreover, 90 per cent of visitors who went to Sydney for the Games are anticipated to become repeat visitors (www.atc.net.au/news/olympic2.htm).

Achieving Celebrity

Image is all-important and how a place is represented can inspire people to visit and revisit it (Coshall, 2000; Tapachai and Waryszak, 2000). Never was the saying 'accentuate the positive and eliminate the negative' more true than in destination branding. Destination marketing requires foresight and planning but it is not an exact science and branding offers destination marketers an opportunity to communicate key place attributes to their intended audience. Branding can help bridge any gaps between a destination's strengths and potential visitors' perceptions. Place reputations are not made in a vacuum and neither are tourist choices, so place marketers must establish how their destination's image compares with those of its key competitors. How the destination rates according to 'wish *you* were here?' appeal and celebrity value is critical. Do tourists regard it as a fashion accessory, a must—see place on every aspirational traveller's shopping list or as a fashion faux pas—somewhere with no conversational value and even less status (Figure 12.1)? Figure 12.2 takes this celebrity matrix and illustrates a range of destination brands measured on the axes of emotional appeal and celebrity value. Obviously, how people relate to any destination brand depends on their own individual interests, opinions and experiences, and such positioning maps must be used in conjunction with psychographic analyses of key market segments.

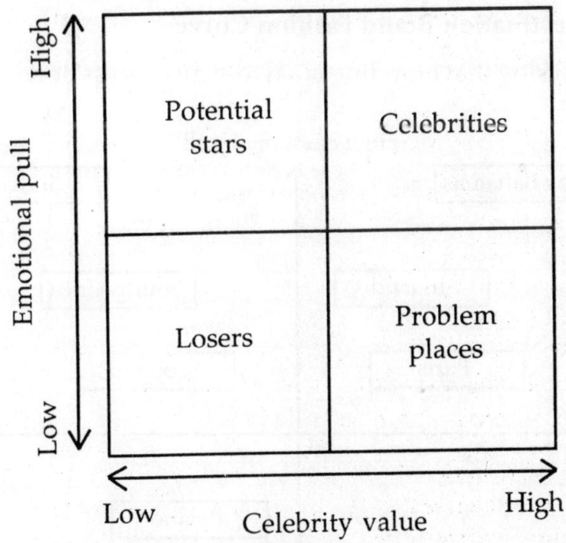

Fig. 12.1. The destination celebrity matrix.

On any positioning map, however, brand winners emerge as those places which are rich in emotional meaning, have great conversation value and hold high anticipation for potential tourists. By comparison, brand losers are places with little meaning, even less status, virtually no conversation value and zero anticipation for tourists. Problem places are those destinations which are talked about for the wrong reasons and, far from holding an emotional appeal, actively repel potential tourists. Places which currently offer little emotional pull face an uphill task if they are ever to become destination winners. Other destinations which do have high emotional pull but currently have limited celebrity value hold huge untapped potential and could be tomorrow's winner destination brands, and currently include places such as India, Cuba, Vietnam and South Africa (Figure 12.2). The challenge for their marketers is to craft identities for these destinations which convey and build on their emotional appeal and which turn them into places with high celebrity value. The message here is that rich, strong destination brands sing a song of difference and have a sense of being somewhere worth visiting.

The Destination Brand Fashion Curve

Recognising that branding is a two-way process done *with* and

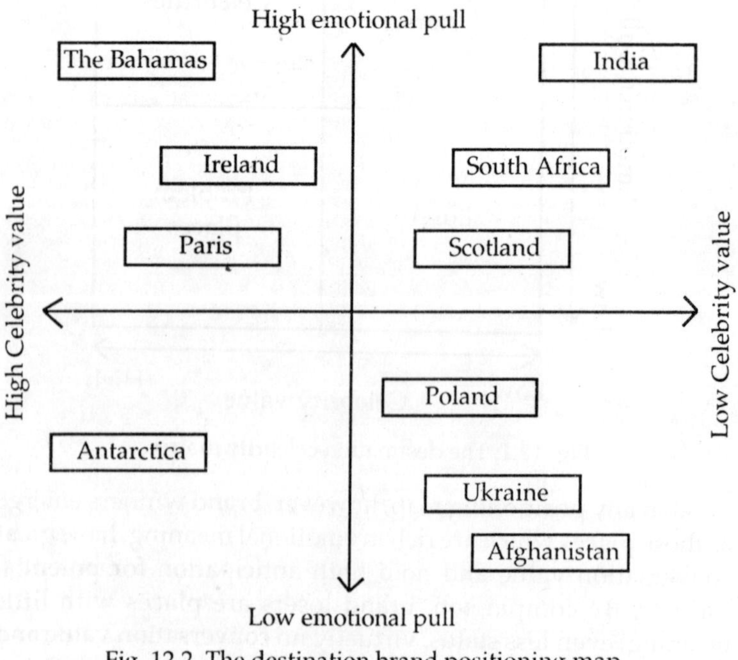

Fig. 12.2. The destination brand positioning map.

not *to* the consumer, Weinreich (1999 : 25-6) has suggested that instead of thinking in terms of the traditional product or brand life cycle, brand managers should be thinking of the S-curve which charts a brand's life and development through birth, growth, maturity, decay and death (although, of course, the time frames are elastic and could encompass anything from weeks to centuries). Instead of seeing the S-curve as tracking sales volume over time, managers should consider it as a series of stages in the brand's relationship with its consumers, revealing useful insights into a brand's communications requirements. Developing this concept and translating it to tourism destination brands, we can see (Figure 12.3) that at first the market is small and many places become trendy in spite of (or due to) their lack of advertising activities because the destination is new and exclusive. Here the destination brand is at the beginning of its fashionable phase and its visitors are trendsetters who, although few in numbers, are influential opinion-formers. Yet, as the destination becomes famous and loses its cutting-edge appeal, these tourists move on to the next new place since they do not want to be seen somewhere which has become popular and rather passé. In the famous phase, a

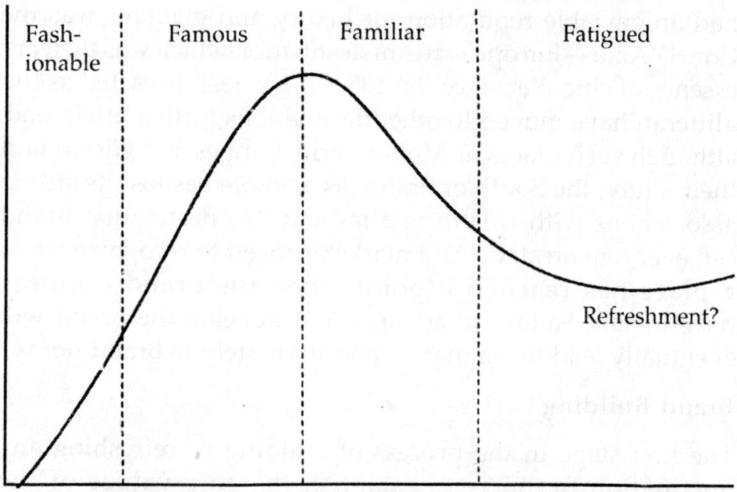

Fig. 12.3. The destination brand fashion curve.

destination brand's consumers are loyal and affluent but at any time the destination's brand values may become irrelevant to them—hence the ongoing need for them to remain fresh and appealing. If the place fails to remain contemporary, it will drift into the familiar zone where everyone knows about the destination, but it has lost its appeal—it has become 'overwarm, cuddly and sentimental, the antithesis of...cool' (Weinreich, 1999 : 28). Becoming familiar can ultimately lead a destination to fatigue—a place which finds it difficult to attract lucerative market segments. If it becomes very badly damaged, a destination brand's core values will need to be reassessed and its relevance to target markets redefined and revitalized.

For every success story such as Ireland and Spain, there are numerous destinations which have become fatally fatigued, having ailed to maintain long term marketing and advertising effort or which have been affected by external change. All brands can show signs of age, needing refreshment in the face of modern competition and even the most classic of brands need to remain contemporary. Certainly, such is the speed of change in today's markets destination brands 'which fail to evolve are brands which will fail. One place which once had an enviable reputation for luxury and glamour was the Cote D'Azur—Europe's dream destination which was the very essence of chic. Yet since the 1950s it has lost its cachet as the glitterati have moved to other destinations further afield and, although such places as Monte Carlo, Cannes and Nice retain their allure, the South of France as a whole has lost its strong associations with wealth and fashion. No destination brand can ever remain static, and marketers need to recognize when a place has reached a point when the brand requires refreshment. Failure to advance and develop the brand will eventually lead to stagnation and ultimately to brand decay.

Brand Building

The first stage in the process of building or refreshing any destination brand is to establish the core values of the destination and its brand—these should be durable, relevant, communicable and hold saliency for potential tourists (Table 12.2). This stage should consider just how contemporary or relevant the brand is to today's tourism consumer and how it compares with its key competitors. For instance, when the Oregon Economic Development Department began its revival of Brand Oregon in the mid-1990s, it initiated a series of research projects which surveyed local businesses, regional economists, other US states with similar programmes and previous visitors—as well as visitors who had never actually been to the state (Curtis, 2001). This process (similar to recent exercises conducted by the brand developers of, among other places, Switzerland, Hawaii, Wales, Western Australia and New Zealand) assisted Oregon's brand managers to build brand value and salience with existing, and potential consumers.

Table 12.2. The Five Phases in Destination Brand Building

Phase One	Market investigation, analysis and strategic recommendations
Phase Two	Brand identity development
Phase Three	Brand launch and introduction—communicating the vision
Phase Four	Brand implementation
Phase Five	Monitoring, evaluation and review

Once this market investigation is complete, the next phase is to develop the brand identity. Of primary importance to this phase are the concepts of the brand benefit pyramid and brand architecture (more of which below). Once the brand's core values have been established, they should underpin and imbue all subsequent marketing activity—especially in literature text and illustrations—so that the brand values are cohesively communicated. A logotype or brand signature and a design style guide, which ensures consistency of message and approach, should also reinforce the brand values. The vision (which must be shared and 'bought into' by all its stakeholders and potential consumers) should be clearly expressed in the brand's core values which are consistently reinforced through the product and in all marketing communications—both above and below the line—every execution in all media contributes to maintaining brand presence. To successfully create an emotional attachment a destination brand has to be :

- credible
- deliverable
- differentiating
- conveying powerful ideas
- enthusing for trade partners
- resonating with the consumer.

A destination which is currently building just such a brand proposition around its stunning natural environment is New Zealand (Harris, 2000; Piggott, 2001). A geographically disadvantaged destination, New Zealand is in the process of building a strong brand to double the country's tourism foreign exchange receipts to more than £3 billion by 2005 (Warren and Thompson, 2000). The '100% Pure New Zealand' campaign, the country's first global marketing campaign, is intended to recover some of the ground lost to Australia in the tourism marketplace (Tourism New Zealand, 2000). The campaign was launched market by market between July 1999 and February 2000 to coincide with seasonal promotional opportunities. Advertising is centred on above-the-line activity; mainly television and print (magazines) and the executions showcase New Zealand's diverse landscapes, people, culture and tourism activities. The key markets for media activity are Australia, Japan, USA, UK, Germany, Singapore and Taiwan—regions which generate the largest number of visitors to New Zealand (Piggott, 2001 : 12).

The '100%' logo incorporates an image of the country's two islands—North and South—while the strap line '100% Pure New Zealand' seeks to position the destination as the ultimate backpacker and thrill-seeker paradise—what the New Zealand brochure describes as a place of 'awesome sights, breathtaking vistas, indelible experiences—that's New Zealand'. The theme of 100 per cent and purity is echoed in all the visuals and the copy of the material, with the scenery, its wines and foods, its people and its experiences being seen as being untainted.

unadulterated, unaffected and undiluted. The brand is intended to position New Zealand as a place (and, indeed, an ethos) shaped by its inhabitants over time. It communicates the quality of the destination's leisure. cultural and heritage products and services, and is the latest step in a strategy to build a clear, consistent and unique identity, building on the New Zealand way and the use of the silver fern. Currently, strap lines such as '100% Pure Romance' and '100% Pure Spirit' are being used. In the long term, M&C Saatchi—the advertising agency responsible for the campaign—is aiming to achieve such consumer awareness of the logo as to be able to drop the '100% New Zealand' strap line and let the '100%' logo stand for Brand New Zealand. The prime targets are so-called 'interactive travellers'—people young in body or heart who love travel, seek new experiences and enjoy the challenge of new destinations. While these consumers are a small proportion of New Zealand's overall tourism market, they are the highly influential opinion-formers who could exert significant influence and make New Zealand a fashionable or famous destination.

Such consumers are often very Web-wise and significantly, the World Wide Web (WWW) is integral to the New Zealand brand, complementing other advertising and public relations activities and media. The destination cyber scene is highly competitive and expensive, and creating and promoting an effective web site is not cheap. The current challenge is for destinations to convert e-browsers into e-buyers and, above all, to match and, where possible, exceed other e-tailer experiences (Morgan, Pritchard and Abbot, 2001). Destinations have to try to convey a sense of experiencing the place (through webcams, weather updates, music clips, oral histories, collection highlights, virtual tours, etc.) and of experiencing the brand rather than merely delivering a site encounter. The New Zealand web site (www.purenz.com) has five attractive 'zones' designed around visitor types and their needs : the wilderness zone (for nature lovers and those who always want to be alone); the thrill zone (for extreme thrill seekers); the heart zone (for visitors who want to meet and stay with real New

Zealanders); the Kiwi spirit zone (for those who want to immerse themselves in New Zealand culture); and the chill out zone (offering relaxing breaks with luxurious accommodation in varied landscapes). This visually attractive site is user friendly and navigable and, above all, stimulates interest and provokes reactions. For instance, web visitors can send copies of the New Zealand adverts and photographs of natural environments as e-postcards—adding to New Zealand's conversational appeal, celebrity and anticipation value.

Brand Personality and the Benefit Pyramid

Critical to the success of the New Zealand brand (as to any other destination brand) is the extent to which the destination's brand personality interacts with the target markets. Just like people, all brands should be complex and rich. In fact, the most powerful brands are those with the richest personalities—we all know how Nike behaves, although (just as if it were a person) we all engage with it in a slightly different way. If a destination brand manager can describe his or her brand on less than a page of A4 paper then the brand personality is nowhere near rich enough to have resonance with the consumer. Yet such complex personalities are quite rare in a world where brand attributes are often arbitrarily and superficially constructed. Traits such as 'friendly', 'cultural', 'natural' and 'contemporary' are popular hoped-for descriptors, but they hardly help to build an engaging or aspirational brand. Destination brand building is all about developing a rich, relevant brand personality. 'Developing' is the key word here—successful brands never atrophy—instead they reflect and respond to changes in consumers' lives and while the brand's core values remain the same, its personality will continue to evolve.

A brand's personality has both a head and a heart—its head refers to the logical brand features, while its heart refers to its emotional benefits and associations. Brand propositions and communications can be based around either a brand's head or its heart : head communications convey a brand's rational values, while heart communications reveal its emotional values and associations. Brand benefit pyramids sum up consumers' relationships with a brand and are frequently established during the consumer research process where consumers are usually asked to describe what features a destination offers and what the place means to them. Using the research, it should then be relatively straightforward to ascertain what particular benefit pyramids consumers associate with the destination in question (see Figure 12.4).

The benefit pyramid can be instrumental in helping to distil the essence of a destination brand's advertising proposition. This refers to the point at which consumers' wants and the destination's benefits and features intersect—any communication (through advertising or public relations) should then encapsulate the *spirit* of the brand. While many ideas may be suggested initially, the challenge is to develop a proposition which makes the destination brand relevant, contemporary and appealing—establishing the brand's architecture can be critical to this process. Thus, for instance, a key element of the new Brand Australia was the creation of a new trademark logo. This was intended to encapsulate the personality and the brand architecture of the destination and

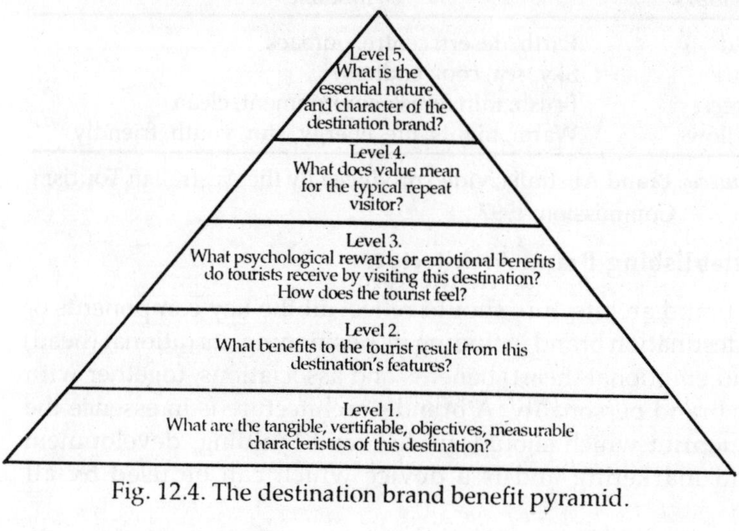

Fig. 12.4. The destination brand benefit pyramid.

had to be bold, exciting, energetic, vital, adventurous and sophisticated yet friendly and fun (Table 12.3). The end result was the creation of a logo depicting a yellow kangaroo against a red sun over a background of green and a blue sea (Table 2.4). The new Australia logo was thus the culmination of a symbol of the country which conveyed the brand personality and included the colours which communicated the architecture.

Table 12.3. The Values and Personality of Brand Australia

Brand values	*Brand Personality*
Youthful	Youthful
Energetic	Stylish
Optimistic	Vibrant
Stylish	Diverse
Unpretentious	Adventurous
Genuine	
Open	
Fun	

Source: Brand Australia, video produced by the Australian Tourism Commission, 1997.

Table 2.4. The Heart of the Australia Logo

Colours	*Symbolize*
Red	Earth, desert, centre, outback
Blue	Sky, sea, cool, endless
Green	Brush, rain forest, environment, clean
Yellow	Warm, nights, life, energy, sun, youth, friendly

Source: Brand Australia, video produced by the Australian Tourism Commission, 1997.

Establishing Brand Architecture

A brand architecture should reflect all the key components of a destination brand including its positioning, its rational (head) and emotional (heart) benefits and associations, together with its brand personality. A brand's architecture is in essence the blueprint which should guide brand building, development and marketing and is a device which can be used by all destination brand managers. More and more tourism destinations are looking to establish their brand architecture in order to put themselves ahead of competitors. Of course, when they are whole countries, destinations are often composite brands (being composed of many different places) Yet consumer research which reveals and establishes a destination's brand architecture should enable marketers to clearly see the elements and contributions of these various composite brands. It is a device critical to the development of *destination suprabrands and sub-brands.* Thus, Britain is a destination suprabrand and the sub-brands (England, Scotland, Wales, London) are both part of, and at the same time, distinct from it (Table 12.5). Thus the *positioning* of Scotland as a land of fire and stone is translated into the *rational benefit* of encountering rugged unspoilt wilderness, romantic history, heritage and folklore, and warm and feisty people. At a deeper, emotional or salient level these benefits offer the overseas visitor the *emotional benefits* of feeling in awe of the elements, embraced by the warmth of the people and rejuvenated by the experience of Scotland. Finally, the culmination of these brand attributes is a destination personified by independence, mystery and warmth. This becomes the essence of *Scotland the Brand,* with values rooted in the experience of past visitors, credible and relevant to potential visitors and, most crucially, which the product can deliver (BTA, 1997).

One of the most successful destination suprabrands, however, must be that of Spain. Once a destination with an image for poor quality service and facilities, in the early 1980s the Spanish government began what was to become one of the most consistent and successful brand-building exercises in destination marketing supported by a significant financial commitment—which is ongoing today (Table 12.6). The suprabrand of Spain is an example of an established destination which attracts 51 million visitors a year and has the world's third largest promotional budget for tourism. While Espana is the main brand, its cities (mainly Barcelona and Madrid) and regions (such as Andalusia and Galicia) are the second-level brands. At the country level Spain has remained remarkably

Table 12.5. The Brand Architecture of Britain

	Positioning	*Rational Benefit*	*Emotional Benefit*	*Personality*
Britain	Island of traditional heritage and the unconventional	Tradition, heritage and pageantry. Landscape. Arts and culture. People	I feel stimulated by the enriching, often paradoxical experience of Britain. I feel at ease in the friendly, open culture of the British people	Great/Solid Yet accessible. Cold in appearance yet deeply friendly. Ordered yet quirky. Traditional yet inovative
London	City of Pageantry and pop	Diverse culture, arts, pageantry, heritage, nightlife, music, glamour, shopping, Safe, cosmopolitan, Fashion leader	I feel liberated by the vibrancy of London, I feel stimulated by the wealth of heritage and culture of a great city	Open-minded. Casual. Unorthodox. Vibrant, Creative
Scotland	Land of fire and stone	Rugged, unspoilt, wilderness, Dramatic scenery, Romantic history, heritage and folklore, Warm and feisty people	I feel in awe of the elements in Scotland. I feel embranced by the warmth of the people. I feel rejuvenated by the experience of Scotland.	Independent. Warm. Mysterious. Rugged. Feisty

(Contd........)

(Contd...)

	Positioning	*Rational Benefit*	*Emotional Benefit*	*Personality*
Wales	Land of nature and legend	Natural, dramatic beauty. Poetry and song. Legend and mystery	I feel inspired by the lyrical beauty of Wales. I feel uplifted by the spirituality of the natural environment.	Honest. Welcoming. Romantic. Down to earth. With passion
England	Lush, green land of discovery	Afternoon teas, quaint village pubs. Cathedrals, country houses. Rolling countryside, meandering roads, hedgerows. Rivers, canals, coastline, piers. Fetes, morris dancing, cricket, rugged country, moorland, lakes. Industrial heritage. Bed and breakfasts, rugby	I feel fulfilled by experiencing the quaint culture and history of England. I feel relaxed by the harmonious countryside and bracing walks along the coast. I feel warmed by the hearty, down-to-earth character of England. I feel soothed by the open, unspoilt outdoors.	Conservative. Pleasant. Refined. Civilized. Eccentric. Down to earth. Approachable. Hearty. Humorous

Source : BTA (1997).

constant in its advertising with each campaign promoting the diversity and variety of the country, focusing on its heritage and culture, as well as the staple sun and sand product. At the heart of the brand for almost twenty years has been Miro's logo, designed in 1983 (the year he died) by mixing elements from his own pictures and his own alphabet. As a piece of modern art, this logo symbolizes Spain's past and looks to the future, and incorporates representations of the sun (yellow and red), the stars and the bullring (black) to portray Spain. The shifts in the campaigns from 'Everything under the sun' (first used in 1984) to 'Passion for Life' (1992-5) to 'Bravo Spain' (introduced in 1997) have been gradual, well thought out and never compromised the brand values. The one departure from this message of passion and diversity came in 1996 when famous photographers were asked to provide their own interpretations of the essence of Spain. A series of posters were created depicting a photograph taken by each photographer with the strap line—for instance, in David Bailey's case—'Spain by Bailey'. While the campaign won several awards for its superb photography, it was disliked by the Spanish tourism industry and proved short-lived.

Table 2.6. Distribution of Spain's Promotional Budget, 1997

Promotional activities	52%
Advertising	43%
Research activities	5%
Total promotional budget	US$71631000

Source: WTO.

The 'Bravo Spain' campaign, which replaced the unpopular 'Spain by ..." campaign of 1996. was tested in the key markets of the UK, Germany and France where it was seen positively—the word 'Bravo' conjured up images of approval—allaying fears in Spain of any negative connotations of its association with bullfighting. Intended to communicate a different, modern Spain, this campaign uses strong, visually impactful images in its television and press and poster executions. In the print advertisements (which are the backbone of the campaign) the consistent image is of a blurred photograph with a larger, perfectly focused close-up window showing some detail of the photograph. Every region of Spain features in the advertisements, which mix well-known attractions (such as the new Bilbao museum) with less well-known sites (such as Valencia's new concert hall), and include interesting copy and a small map indicating the location of the scene in the poster.

Conclusion

The success of countries like Spain shows that destinations can become brands which are contemporary and yet timeless, and which can remain in the famous phase of their brand fashion curve over a prolonged period of time. That does not mean, however, that it is easy to build a strong place brand. It takes patience to establish brand reputations and building a powerful destination brand requires a long-term effort, which more often than not yields incremental and not exponential results. Of course, there are destination brands which have seemingly emerged from obscurity to achieve instant stardom. Such rapid elevation to celebrity status, however, often owes much to a culmination of long-term economic, political, social and cultural factors. The apparently effortless appearance of Ireland as a cool, fashionable destination, for instance, is the result of over twenty year of economic turnaround, coupled with the breakthorough of Irish culture (especially the performing arts) on to the world stage. Often such instant stardom also belies long-term marketing activity and investment built on detailed marketing research, planning and consistent positioning. Ireland has continuously inverted heavily in product development and in its marketing activities, and today considerably outspends all of its competitor UK destinations in the key markets.

Certainly, those destinations which have emerged as brand winners do have a number of common features—in addition to being well funded. They have all been based on a vision which is founded on intensive stakeholder, consumer and competitor research, and which is expressed with care and discipline in everything which communicates the brand's personality. Many have set out to be inclusive brands, forged through partnership and alliance, and many are spear headed by forward-looking, innovative and commited managers. The commitment and energy of such 'brand champions' is a vital but often overlooked ingredient in any successful destination branding strategy. Such people could be influential politicians or they could be brand envisioners drawn from the destination's marketing organization. This is not to say, however, that the branding should be exclusively directed from the 'top down' and we have seen how this can be counterproductive—as in the case of Oregon in the mid-1980s. The best brands are those which are flexible and inclusive with a broad base of support. Indeed, the development of such partnerships is often a beneficial spin-off from destination brand-building activities, creating greater cohesion between tourism marketers and economic development agencies (Crockett and Wood, 1999; Curtis, 2001).

In addition to being well supported by internal stakeholders, those destination brands which have the greatest celebrity value also tend to be those who produce good advertising. The choice of advertising agency is crucial here since they must produce advertising which advances the brand and reinforces its values and personality. Successful destination brands usually have consistent, relevant, appealing and high-quality advertising, characterized by high production values advertising which is often cutting-edge advertising and extremely creative. This is not to suggest, however, that destination brand managers must not be prepared to adjust misdirected communications. Spain showed that swift action to correct an unpopular expression of the brand's personality (the 1996 'Spain by ...' campaign) can prevent long term-damage to the brand. Continuous monitoring and evaluation of the communications is the key here, as is open-mindedness and a willingness to embrace change on the part of the brand managers.

Any change must be managed within the overall consistency of the brand of course. Once the brand personality has been identified, marketers must have if courage to stay with the brand's essence—while refinements may be made to how the values are expressed in the brand architecture, the essentials of the brand personality should remain consistent. The secret is to continually evolve and enrich the original brand personality, building on the initial strengths to increase their appeal and to broaden the market. Oregon, for instance, took its established reputation as a pristine natural environment and enriched the brand's personality but including a focus on the destination's built environment and its cultural attractions (Curtis, 2001). This is similar to the strategy adopted by Spain, which wove culture, heritage and an emerging reputation for modern architecture into its original brand personality based around sun and sand. Likewise Ireland has added culture, 'coolness' and quality to its established identity as a laid back, friendly destination and Australia has added sophistication and a cosmopolitan dimension to its youthful, fun, nature-oriented personality.

There are significant and unique problems facing destination marketers but these should not prevent them from persevering in their aims—successful branding brings enormous rewards. Certainly, destinations cannot afford to ignore branding as in offers an innovative and effective tool by which managers can establish emotional links with the consumer, particularly if a multiagency-driven suprabrand is constructed. Just as in the marketing of consumer goods, branding has the potential to engender consumer loyalty and position destinations to appeal to consumers self images and lifestyles. Moreover, while tourism is just one element of any, destination's economy it should be integral to place marketing since it supports and leads the development of a place brand. The creation of celebrity and emotional appeal through a destination brand opens the way for other economic development-oriented agencies to communicate to would-be investors and residents.

REFERENCES

Anholt, S. (1998). Nation-brands of the twenty-first century. *Journal of Brand Management,* **5(6)**, 395-404.

Baloglu, S. and Brinberg, D. (1997). Affective images of tourism destinations. *Journal of Travel Research,* **4,** Spring, 11-14

British Tourist Authority (BTA) (1997). *Living Britain, A Guide to Understanding the Characteristics of the Geographic Brands of Britain, London, Scotland, England and Wales.* BTA.

Buhalis. D. (2000). Marketing the competitive destination of the future. *Tourism Management,* **21**(91), 97-116.

Chernatony, L. de (1993). Categorising brands : evolutionary processes underpinned by two key dimensions. *Journal of Marketing Management,* **9**(2).

Coshall, J. T. (2000). Measurement of tourists' images : the repertory grid approach. *Journal of Travel Research,* **39**(1), 85-89.

Crockett, S. R. and Wood, L. J. (1999). 'Brand Western Australia : a totally integrated approach to destination branding. *Journal of Vacation Marketing,* **5**(3), 276-289.

Curtis, J. (2001). Branding a state : the evolution of Brand Oregon. *Journal of Vacation Marketing,* **7**(1), 75-82.

Garfield, R. (1998). Personal interview.

Hall, D. (1999). Destination branding, niche marketing and national image projection in central and Eastern Europe. *Journal of Vacation Marketing,* **5**(3), 227-237.

Hallberg, G. (1995). *All Consumers Are Not Created Equal.* Wiley.

Harris, C. (2000). New Zealand's 100% Pure campaign : the UK market. Unpublished paper presented at UWIC, November, 2000.

Lurman, D. (of the World Tourism Organization) (1998). Presentation at the 1998 International Travel and Tourism Awards, Valencia.

Lury, G. (1998). *Brandwatching.* Blackball.

Macrae, C. Parkinson S. and Sheerman, J. (1995). Managing marketing's DNA : the role of branding. *Irish Marketing Review,* **18**, 13-20.

Morgan, N. J. and Pritchard, A. (1998). *Tourism Promotion and Power : Creating Images, Creating Identities.* Wiley.

Morgan, N. J. and Pritchard, A. (1999). Building destination brands : the cases of Wales and Australia. *Journal of Brand Management,* 7(2), 102-119.

Morgan, N.J. and Pritchard, A. (2000). *Advertising in Tourism and Leisure.* Butterworth-Heinemann.

Morgan, N. J., Pritchard, A. and Abbot, S. (2001). Consumers, travel and technology : a bright future for the Web or television shopping? *Journal of Vacation Marketing,* 7(2), April, 110-124.

Morse, J. (2001). The Sydney 2000 Olympic Games : how the Australian Tourist Commission leveraged the games for tourism', *Journal of Vacation Marketing,* 7(2), 101-109.

Nickerson, N. P. and Moisey, N. R. (1999). Branding a state from features to positioning : making it simple? *Journal of Vacation Marketing,* **5**(3), 217-226.

Piggott, R. (2001). Building a brand for a country. Can commercial marketing practices achieve this in a government-funded environment? Unpublishes University of Hull MBA dissertation.

Ritchie, B.J.R. and Crouch, G. I. (2000). The competitive destination : a sustainable prespective. *Tourism Management,* **21**(1), 1-7.

Rodwell, T. (1999). Presentation at the 1999 International Travel and Tourist Awards, Valencia.

Schiffman, L. G. and Kanuk, L. L. (2000). *Consumer Behaviour.* 7th edn., Printed Hall International.

Sheth, J. N., Mittal, B. and Newman, B. I. (1999). *Customer Behaviour*: Consumer Behaviour and Beyond, Dryden Press.

Tapachai, N. and Waryszak, R. (2000). An examination of the role of beneficial image in tourist destination selection. *Journal of Travel Research,* **39**(I), August, 37-44.

Tibbott, R. (2001). Olympic economies : Sydney and the destination economy. *Locum Destination Review,* **3,** 33-34.

Tourism New Zealand (TNZ) (2000). *Growing New Zealand's Share of the UK Travel Market,* TNZ.

Urdde, M. (1999). Brand orientation : a mindset for building brands into strategic resources. *Journal of Marketing Management*, **15** (1-3), 117-133.

Vial, C. (of Publicis) (1997). Paper presented at the first International Leisure and Tourism Advertising Awards, Dubrovnik.

Warren, S. and Thompson, W. (2000). New Zealand 100% Pure. *Locum Destination Review*, **1**, 22-26.

Weinreich, L. (1999). 11 *Steps to Brand Heaven : The Ultimate Guide to Buying an Advertising Campaign*, Kogan Page.

Westwood, S., Morgan, N. J., Pritchard, A. and Ineson, E. (1999). Branding the package holiday : the role and significance of brands for UK air tour operators. *Journal of Vacation Marketing*, 5(3), July, 238-252.

www.atc.net.au/news/olympic2.htm (accessed 28 February 2001).

BIBLIOGRAPHY

All Parts

Medlik, S. (1996). *Dictionary of Travel, Tourism and Hospitality*, 2nd edn, Oxford : Butterworth-Heinemann.

Chapter 2—Anatomy of Tourism

Burkart, A.J. and Medlik, S. (1981). *Tourism—Past, Present and Future,* 2nd edn, London : Heinemann, chs. 4 and 5.

McIntosh, R., Goeldner, C. and Ritchie, B. (1995). *Tourism : Principles, Practices, Philosophies,* 7th edn, New York : John Wiley.

World Tourism Organization (1993). *Recommendations on Tourism Statistics,* New York : United Nations.

United Nations/World Tourism Organization (1995). *Recommendations on Tourism Statistics,* New York : United Nations.

Chapter 3—Historical Development of Tourism

Burkart, A.J. and Medlik, S. (1990). *Historical Development of Tourism,* Less Cahiers du Tourisme Serie C No. 143, Aix-en-Provence : Centre des Hautes Etudes Touristiques.

Holloway, J.C. (1994). *The Business of Tourism,* 4th edn., London : Pitman, chs. 2 and 3.

Towner, J. (1996). *An Historical Geography of Recreation and Tourism in the Western World 1540-1940,* Chichester : John Wiley.

Chapter 4—Geography of Tourism

Boniface, B.G. and Cooper, C.P. (1994). *The Geography of Travel and Tourism,* 2nd edn., Oxford : Butterworth-Heinemann.

Hudman, L.E. and Jackson, R.H. (1994). *Geography of Travel and Tourism,* 2nd edn., Albany, NY : Delmar Publishers.

Pearce, D. (1995). *Tourism Today : A Geographical Analysis,* 2nd edn., Harlow : Longman.

Chapter 5—Dimensions of Tourism

British Tourist Authority (intermittent). *Digest of Tourism Statistics,* London : BTA.

Cooper, C., Fletcher, J., Gilbert, D. and Wanhill, S. (1993). *Tourism : Principles and Practice,* London : Pitman, chs. 6 and 7.

Tourism Works for America Council (annual). *Tourism Works for America Annual Report,* Washington, DC.

United Nations/World Tourism Organization (1995). *Recommendations on Tourism Statistics,* New York : United Nations.

World Tourism Organization (annual). *Compendium of Tourism Statistics,* Madrid : WTO.

See also text for particular statistical sources.

Chapter 6—Significance of Tourism

Bull, A. (1995). *The Economics of Travel and Tourism,* 2nd edn., Harlow : Longman.

Cooper, C., Fletcher, J., Gilbert, D. and Wanhill, S. (1993). *Tourism : Principles and Practice,* London : Pitman, chs. 10 and 11.

Mathieson, A. and Wall, G. (1982). *Tourism : Economic, Physical and Social Impacts,* Harlow : Longman.

Fridgen, J.D. (1991). *Dimensions of Tourism,* East Lansing, MI : Educational Institute of American Hotel & Motel Association, chs. 4, 6, 7.

Tourism Works for America Council (annual) *Tourism Works for America Annual Report,* Washington, DC.

Chapter 7—The Tourism Industry

Cooper, C., Fletcher, J., Gilbert, D. and Wanhill, S. (1993). *Tourism : Principles and Practice,* London : Pitman, chs. 15-18.

Holloway, J.C. (1994). *The Business of Tourism,* 4th edn., London : Pitman, chs. 7-13.

Medlik, S. (1994). *The Business of Hotels,* 3rd edn., Oxford : Butterworth-Heinemann.

Swarbrooke, J. (1995). *The Development and Management of Visitor Attractions,* Oxford : Butterworth-Heinemann.

Tourism Works for America Council (annual). *Tourism Works for America Annual Report,* Washington, DC.

Chapter 8—Marketing in Tourism

Middleton, V.T.C (1994). *Marketing in Travel and Tourism,* 2nd edn., Oxford : Butterworth-Heinemann.

Morrison, A.M. (1989). *Hospitality and Travel Marketing,* Albany, NY : Delmar Publishers.

Witt, S.F. and Moutinho, L. (eds) (1994). *Tourism Marketing and Management Handbook,* 2nd edn., Part III, Hemel Hempstead : Prentice Hall.

Chapter 9—Planning and Development in Tourism

Gunn, C.A. (1994). *Tourism Planning : Basics, Concepts, Cases,* 3rd edn, Washington DC : Taylor Francis.

Innskeep, E. (1994). *National and Regional Tourism Planning—Methodologies and Case Studies,* London : Routledge.

Pearce, D. (1989). *Tourist Development,* 2 edn., Harlow : Longman.

Chapter 10—Organization and Finance in Tourism

Burkart, A.J. and Medlik, S. (1981). *Tourism – Past, Present and Future,* 2nd edn., London : Heinemann, Part IX.

Hollier, R. (1995). *The National and Regional Structure of Official Tourist Organisations in European Communities,* Paris : European Travel Commission.

Pearce, D. (1992). *Tourist Organizations,* Harlow : Longman.

Chapter 11—Miscellaneous Topics

Khan, M., Olsen, M. and Var, T. (eds.) (1993). *VNR's Encyclopaedia of Hospitality and Tourism,* New York : Van Nostrand Reinhold.

Medlik, S. (ed.) (1995). *Managing Tourism,* Oxford : Butterworth-Heinemann.

Seaton, A. V. (ed.) (1995). *Global Tourism : The Next Decade,* Oxford : Butterworth-Heinemann.

Witt, S.F. and Moutinho, L. (eds) (1994). *Tourism Marketing and Management Handbook,* 2nd edn., Hemel Hempstead : Prentice Hall.

